Reimbursement for Athletic Trainers

Reimbursement for Athletic Trainers

Marjorie Albohm, MS, ATC
Orthopaedics Indianapolis
Indianapolis, Indiana

with

Dan Campbell, PT, ATC
Mayo Clinic
Rochester, Minnesota

Jeff G. Konin, MEd, ATC, MPT
Delaware Technical and Community College
Georgetown, Delaware

An innovative information, education and management company
6900 Grove Road • Thorofare, NJ 08086

Publisher: John H. Bond
Editorial Director: Amy E. Drummond
Editorial Assistant: William J. Green

The procedures and practices described in this book should be implemented in a manner consistent with the professional standards set for the circumstances that apply in each specific situation. Every effort has been made to confirm the accuracy of the information presented and to correctly relate gen-erally accepted practices. The author, editor, and publisher cannot accept responsibility for errors or exclusions or for the outcome of the application of the material presented herein. There is no expressed or implied warranty of this book or information imparted by it.

The work SLACK publishes is peer reviewed. Prior to publication, recognized leaders in the field, educators, and clinicians provide important feedback on the concepts and content that we publish. We welcome feedback on this work.

Printed in the United States of America.

Albohm, Marjorie J.
    Reimbursement for athletic trainers / Marjorie Albohm, Dan Campbell, Jeff G. Konin.
       p. cm. -- (Athletic training library)
    Includes bibliographical references and index.
    ISBN 1-55642-408-6 (alk. paper)
     1. Insurance, Health--United States. 2. Athletic trainers--United States. I. Campbell,
Dan. II. Konin, Jeff G. III. Title. IV. Series

RA413.5.U5 A5334 2001
258.2'00973--dc21

                                                                2001020075

Published by: SLACK Incorporated
                     6900 Grove Road
                     Thorofare, NJ 08086 USA
                     Telephone: 856-848-1000
                     Fax: 856-853-5991
                     www.slackbooks.com

Last digit is print number: 10   9   8   7   6   5   4   3   2   1

DEDICATION

To certified athletic trainers, whose belief in themselves and the value of their skills has established their role as essential health care providers in the reimbursable arena.

CONTENTS

Dedication v

Acknowledgments ix

About the Authors xi

Preface xiii

Foreword xv

Chapter One   Third-Party Reimbursement in American Health Care 1

Chapter Two   Athletic Training and Third-Party Reimbursement 11

Chapter Three   The National Athletic Trainers' Association Reimbursement
Advisory Group 19

Chapter Four   The Basics of Claims Filing 37

Chapter Five   Reimbursement for Athletic Trainers by Practice Setting 55

Chapter Six   Reimbursement Strategies 75

Chapter Seven   The Future 83

Appendix 1   National Athletic Trainers' Association Approach to Payer Guidelines 89

Appendix 2   Medicare, CPT Codes, and UB Code Rulings 95

Appendix 3   Fact Sheet on Athletic Training and the National Athletic
Trainers' Association 99

Appendix 4   An Outcomes Assessment of Care Provided by Certified
Athletic Trainers 103

Appendix 5   Request for Proposals—Athletic Training Outcomes Assessment
Data 113

Appendix 6   Improve Your Bottom Line with Certified Athletic Trainers 119

Appendix 7   Letter of Support 123

Appendix 8   The National Athletic Trainers' Association: Certified Athletic
Trainers—Unique Health Care Providers 125

Appendix 9   The State of Georgia, House Bill 93 127

Appendix 10   Billing Vignettes 133

Glossary 137

Index 143

ACKNOWLEDGMENTS

To the contributing authors, Dan Campbell and Jeff Konin, whose expertise added essential components to this book.

The original members of the National Athletic Trainers' Association (NATA) Reimbursement Advisory Group (RAG) whose visionary leadership set the stage for all future accomplishments.

Joe Godek, who first brought "outcomes" to our attention and made us realize its importance.

The NATA board of directors who have steadfastly and enthusiastically supported the initiatives and activities of the RAG, and who have put their trust and confidence in our efforts.

Rich Rogers, NATA Manager of Governmental Relations and Reimbursement, who provides tireless support to the activities of the RAG and, who shares our vision for the future.

Teresa Foster-Welsh, NATA Director of Marketing and Communications who provided needed energy and expertise at the most critical times.

Dan Campbell, ATC, PT and Keith Webster, MA, ATC, my trusted advisers who always believed that we could achieve the impossible—and we did!

Amy Drummond, SLACK Editorial Director, whose commitment to athletic training made this series and this book possible. Thank you for your personal support and friendship and for advancing the profession of athletic training.

ABOUT THE AUTHORS

Marjorie J. Albohm received her BS degree from Valparaiso University and her MS degree from Indiana State University. She was one of the first women in the nation certified by NATA. She is the author of the book, *Health Care and the Female Athlete*, and coauthor of the book, *Your Injury: A Common Sense Guide to Sports Injuries.*

Ms. Albohm was the first chairperson of the NATA RAG and has served in that position since 1995. She is the former president of the NATA Research and Education Foundation and a former member of the NATA Convention Committee. She currently serves on the NATA board of directors as District 4 Director.

Ms. Albohm is a 1999 inductee into the NATA Hall of Fame and is a recipient of the "Tim Kerin Award for Excellence in Athletic Training" as well as the NATA "Most Distinguished Athletic Trainer" award. Currently she is Director of Sports Medicine and Orthopaedic Research at Orthopaedics Indianapolis, Indianapolis, Indiana.

Dan Campbell holds a BS degree and a certificate in physical therapy from the University of Iowa. He is employed as the Coordinator of Athletic Training at the Mayo Clinic in Rochester, Minnesota. Mr. Campbell has served on the NATA Governmental Affairs Committee, RAG, and Council on Employment. He was awarded the "Most Distinguished Athletic Trainer" award in 1996.

Jeff G. Konin is a graduate of Eastern Connecticut State University, the University of Virginia, and the University of Delaware. He has been involved with NATA as a member of the Clinical/Industrial/Corporate committee, the RAG, and as the liaison to the American Physical Therapy Association (APTA). Mr. Konin has previously edited *Special Tests for Orthopedic Examination, Clinical Athletic Training,* and *Practical Kinesiology for the PTA,* all published by SLACK, Incorporated. Currently Mr. Konin is an instructor at Delaware Technical and Community College in Georgetown, Delaware and the president of Coastal Health Consultants, P.A., Lewes, Delaware.

PREFACE

Health care has changed dramatically in recent years and that change has caused payers, providers, and patients to assess and critique the health care delivery system from every aspect. The restructuring of our health care system has created opportunities for formerly unknown providers to demonstrate their skills and value and compete for their share of the health care dollar.

The profession of athletic training has changed over the last 10 to 15 years almost as dramatically as health care itself. Once almost exclusively employed by educational institutions and professional sports teams, 40% of today's certified athletic trainers are employed in clinical settings treating athletes and people of all ages involved in physical activity. From the youth sports participant, to the weekend warrior, to the industrial worker, athletic trainers are providing effective and valued services to these varied populations.

Unlike the educational setting, the clinical setting operates on a system of third-party payer reimbursement, something few ATC's were ever schooled in. To establish and maintain employment in these settings on an equal basis with other allied health care providers, it is evident that ATC's must be recognized, accepted, and valued as reimbursable entities.

Pursuing reimbursement for athletic trainers is no longer a choice, as it was in 1995 when the NATA Board of Directors voted to form the reimbursement advisory group (RAG). It is a necessity for the future growth of our profession. Soon not only will clinically employed athletic trainers be effected by reimbursement, but also those in the educational setting as already evidenced.

Change creates opportunity and we as athletic trainers are faced with the greatest opportunity in our history—to demonstrate our skills and value to the health care world and become accepted, respected, reimbursable health care providers, to share those skills and benefits that athletes have long realized and appreciated with the physically active public, to proudly stake our claim to a share of the health care market, and to firmly secure our present and our future.

This book is the first ever written specifically to address reimbursement for athletic trainers. It is the first of many books that will be written on this subject because we have so much more to learn and accomplish. Chapters One through Three chronicle the history of third-party reimbursement in American health care and the history of the NATA and athletic training in third-party reimbursement. Chapters Four and Five describe the basics of claims filing, the use of regulatory codes, and focus on reimbursement for athletic trainers by practice setting. Chapters Six and Seven outline the goals and strategies for the immediate and not-so-distant future. The appendices contain a wealth of related information needed to understand the reimbursement process for athletic training.

Health care certainly hasn't stopped changing and no one can or will predict what the final outcome will be. One thing will remain constant, however: that the services provided by certified athletic trainers are recognized as beneficial, valuable, sought after, and reimbursable.

FOREWORD

Individuals, groups, and state athletic trainer associations have taken an active role in seeking reimbursement for athletic training services. Direct and indirect reimbursement continue to grow across the country. Legal decisions, legislative activity, and interpretations at the state and federal level have fueled this movement, while setbacks have only intensified this activity.

Athletic trainers have woked in a budget capped, managed care environment in the traditional training room setting for over 50 years. Those employed in nontraditional settings such as clinics, hospitals, and industrial environments continue to practice the same skills on very similar injuries and illnesses. Outcomes studies have validated the value of athletic trainers in all settings.

The one constant in medicine and society today is change. Our ability to embrace change will lead to future success in the reimbursement arena. This text is a testimony to the steep learning curve and the ability of the authors and their colleagues to be forward thinkers, visualizing the future and not accepting failure as the truth.

Thomas E. Koto, Jr, ATC/ATR

Chapter One

Third-Party Reimbursement in American Health Care

OBJECTIVES

Following the completion of this chapter, the reader will be able to:
- Trace the history of health care reimbursement in the United States.
- Identify the origin and development of major commercial third-party payers.
- Trace the development and organization of managed care.
- Identify and understand government health insurance plans.

HISTORY OF REIMBURSEMENT

As in many social patterns found in American history, the concept of third-party reimbursement for health care has its roots in Europe. Anderson notes that in 1883, Otto von Bismarck established a compulsory health insurance program on a national basis in Germany.[1] The program was designed to assist workers earning less than a threshold income with health care costs. The program was administered by workers themselves through "sickness" societies and paid for physician services, medications, glasses, and hospitalizations.[1] Enzmann, on the contrary, viewed such reimbursements as wage protections for the bread winner.[2] The program was funded by deductions from wages and mandatory contributions by employers. Sickness or "benefit" societies were self-help associations, organized and funded by workers, and were separated by trade industries.[1] The program was not well received, as only 10% of the population was covered.[1] There was little physician opposition to the program initially since German physicians were not organized in their own right at the time. The major opposition came from the employers who thought that having workers' societies administer the reimbursement process would lead to excessive costs and poor results.[1]

Early in American history, reimbursement for health care costs was strictly an individual burden. Governments appeared not to be interested in interfering with personal decisions in health care. The state of health care was primitive as compared to the European model. In America, physicians were predominately trained through the apprenticeship method until the late 19th century[1] and had not been required to be licensed until a few decades earlier.[2] Until then, physicians were seen as little more than charlatans, and hospitals had no more value than charnel houses. Fees were set by the physician and payment was negotiated on an individual basis, often on a barter system. This was typical of the fee-for-service concept in American health care. But, the ideas that eventually led to the formation of the American health insurance industry were already in development.

According to Enzmann, the foundation of insurance is to create better access to health care for the middle class.[3] The early years of American health were marked by the presence of the Blue Cross plans. The Blue Cross concept was originally started in 1929 in Dallas, Tex, as hospital insurance for school teachers.[4] Both Blue Cross and Blue Shield plans were provider-sponsored (Blue Cross by hospitals and Blue Shield by physicians) and were sold either to employers or to employees. Soon the Blues were challenged by other commercial carriers.[3] The major difference between the Blues and the other companies lay in the use of rating systems to determine insurance premiums or the cost of the policy to the employer/employee. The Blues used a concept called the "community rating," and the other companies used "experience rating."[3] In both methods, the purpose was to determine the amount needed by the carrier to cover expected claims and administrative costs and return a profit. Community rating methods relied on applying a standard rate to all groups within the community and then adding on tiers of extra charges based on other parameters. These parameters might have included marital status, dependents, lifestyle, etc. Experience rating methodology relied on past history with groups of similar characteristics. Premiums were then developed and offered to the purchaser. By using experience ratings, in particular, other carriers were able to offer lower premiums to employers.[3] In general, the reimbursement strategy was the same for all carriers—reimburse the provider for the services rendered.[3] Initially, insurance companies did little more than collect premiums, process invoices for payment, and increase their profit margin by increasing the numbers of employers that they served. The fee-for-service indemnity plans did not impose any cost controls on the providers. These plans may have influenced providers to do more for their patients than may have been necessary since the providers were going to be paid more.

Prepaid health care plans, now known as managed care products, have also been in existence for several decades. By the early 1900s, prepaid or company-based plans were being used by companies for employees in isolated regions. Dr. Sidney Garfield began one of the first plans for the employees of Henry J. Kaiser, who was building the Grand Coulee dam.[3] Kaiser saw the plan as a fringe benefit that would keep valued workers in the area longer and in better health while on the job. The thought was that guaranteed health care would keep productivity high. Kaiser espoused the idea again in the 1940s as a method to keep skilled workers in his shipyards and steel mills.[3] Prepaid or company-based medical programs for workers were opposed by the American Medical Association (AMA). The fledgling AMA saw physician-employees losing their autonomy in determining appropriate treatment protocols and jeopardizing the ability of all physicians to set their own fees. Early company physician-employees were expelled from the AMA and local medical societies and were barred from privileges at local community hospitals.[3] While Kaiser is generally credited with opening up the pre-paid health insurance concept to the general public in 1945,[3] a rural cooperative health plan started in Elk City, Okla, in 1929 may be the oldest health maintenance organization (HMO) in America.[4] West coast middle class individuals joined the new HMOs in sufficient numbers that ensured the continuation of the newer concept.

Hospital involvement in reimbursement followed a more circuitous path. The first hospitals in America were sponsored by religious orders, by local community boards, or by philanthropists.[1] These hospitals were required by their charters to treat the poor. It was not until the time that anesthesia and antisepsis were used that the public recognized the value of surgery.[1] Surgery led to agreements with local physicians to allow admission of their patients, which in turn, promoted the use of hospitals as sites of treatment as opposed to the reputation of the past. Wealthy private patients paid for the services rendered by the hospital separately from those services provided for by the physician.[1] Those fees allowed the hospitals to serve greater numbers of needy patients. In addition, the agreements with physicians called for the physicians to treat poor patients as well.[1]

THE INFLUENCE OF THE FEDERAL GOVERNMENT

In the mid 20th century, the United States passed three laws that fundamentally changed health care in this country. During World War II, Congress enacted wage freezes. In order to keep the unions mollified, Congress did allow employers to exempt certain fringe benefits, including pension plans and health insurance, from corporate income tax liability. Thus, companies could offer increased health care benefits when they could not increase wages.[1] In a relatively short period of time, no doubt bolstered by the return of service men and women from the war to the industrial setting, employer-purchased health insurance became an expected entitlement for employment. That led to a phenomenon noticed in the 1950s. In just a little more than 30 years, more than half of the population of the country changed from paying for its own health care to being covered by a third-party payer.[1] That type of phenomenon would rise again in the 1990s.

In 1946, Congress passed the Hospital Survey and Construction Act, also known as the Hill-Burton Act. The purpose of the act was to cause state governments to survey their health care needs with respect to hospitals and to stimulate construction of hospitals in rural areas.[1] The method used was through offering grants, to be matched by the hospitals themselves, for start-up construction costs.[1] The federal grants spurred the interest of the wealthy public for philanthropy and, since the act did not discriminate between public and private operations, expansion of the number of hospital beds in each state soon reached the maximum threshold of 4.5 beds per 1000 citizens.[5] Filling those beds became the responsibility of physicians, and they were underwritten by the insurance companies. A cash cow was created and providers were able to order as many tests or to perform as many procedures as possible. Eventually, this type of unrestricted fee-for-services system would lead to the double-digit annual increases in medical costs created in the 1980s. Cost controls were still a long way off in the future.

Until the mid 1960s, however, the federal government did not actively try to influence health care cost reimbursements. The federal government had maintained its own medical system for its armed services veterans but had kept away from controlling reimbursement of medical costs. In 1965, both the Medicare and Medicaid Acts were passed. The former was intended to assist the elderly with health care costs, and the latter was meant to assist states with health care of the poor.[1] Both of these acts firmly entrenched governments as payers for health care. Medicare and Medicaid expenditures by the federal government totaled 16% of the budget in 1994.[4]

In the past decade, spurred on by the ill-fated health care reform plan proposed by President Clinton, the insurance industry has undergone a rather startling transformation. Realizing that health care costs were continually climbing in America at a rate of 20%[6] and realizing that employer-purchasers of insurance were balking at increased premium costs (in 1997, health care costs were 13.9% of the gross domestic product),[3] the industry reformed itself by ratcheting down its reimbursement to providers. The traditional indemnity plan product, wherein the provider of services is compensated for the cost of the service plus a profit (at usual, customary, and reasonable [UCR] rates) has been discarded for a managed care product line that emphasizes shared risk. Indemnity plans that once covered 62% of workers in 1991 covered 27% in 1995.[6] Managed care products have taken up the difference. In 1993, managed care organization (MCO) plans covered 52% of all workers, and by 1997, MCO plans enrolled 85%.[7] It is possible that managed care held down the growth in health care spending for a short time. Health care spending increases dropped from 5% in 1993 and held steady at just over 2% for the following 3 years before rebounding to over 3% in 1997.[8] Even then, average premium costs fell 5.8% for indemnity plans and fell 0.15% for MCO plans in 1997.[7]

MANAGED CARE ORGANIZATIONS

MCOs can be seen as managed access organizations. Enrollees in MCO plans give up the illusion of choice of providers for their health care. Despite the insurance industry's resounding defeat of the Clinton health care proposal through a masterful advertising campaign that highlighted loss of choice in providers, health care in America has always been limited in access to providers. First, by geography with the level of rural health care often being inferior to the level of urban health care. Second, by cost with the wealthy being able to pay for services universally unavailable to the poor. Third, by limited availability of specialty providers who were concentrated in urban or academic centers. MCOs have put a different spin on the accessibility issue by limiting the choice of providers from the beginning. Enrollees are required to pick their providers from a roster of physicians and allied health practitioners that is contracted by the MCO to render services to its clients.

MCOs have three hallmarks that differentiate them from other medical care establishments. MCOs:

1. Promote use of a physician gatekeeper
2. Emphasize cost reduction through various methods
3. Demand provider accountability

While other medical care entities may use some of the same techniques to control costs, MCOs are unique in that their primary purpose is to offer a less expensive health care product. In exchange, purchasers (whether employers or individuals) realize a level of care that is less expansive than the traditional fee-for-service model. In the fee-for-service model, more services provided for a patient resulted in higher total reimbursements for the provider, which in turn lead to increased utilization of services that may not have been necessary.

Managed Care Revenues

Ward[4] states that premiums are the result of an underwriting procedure by the MCO. The underwriting procedure evaluates the demographic data of the client group (age, sex, work environment, etc) along with health policies of the employer (if the employer is the purchaser) and the competition for the business. The underwriting procedure results in a rate calculation. It is important to remember that MCO premiums are prepaid for the succeeding time period and are effective whether or not services covered by the premium are actually used. Premiums are the primary source of revenue for MCOs. A second source of revenue is coordination of benefits.[4] If the MCO is the primary benefit payer, then in the presence of another insurance policy, the MCO still bears the brunt of the medical care costs. Should the MCO act as a secondary payer, then it is important that the primary carrier benefits be utilized completely prior to the benefits of the MCO being used. A third source of revenue for the MCO is reinsurance recoveries. Reinsurance is purchased by the MCO to protect against high-cost claims. In case of high-cost claims, after a deductible amount is covered by the MCO, the reinsurance policy pays a portion of the costs. Another source of income is interest from money collected from pre-paid premiums but held for 30 days before being paid out for claims.

Managed Care Expenses

The expense side of the income sheet for MCOs is comprised primarily by payouts for medical benefits. According to Ward,[4] medical benefits include (with percentage of total expenses for a typical MCO):

- Inpatient (28%)
- Outpatient (11%)
- Primary care services (12%)
- Specialty care (20%)
- Ancillary services, such as laboratory and radiology (15%)
- Prescription drugs (9%)
- Other services (5%)

As one can see, inpatient services are far more expensive than outpatient services. MCOs attempt to control costs by offering incentives to provider organizations to use more outpatient services than inpatient. MCOs also spread the risk of benefit payouts to primary care practitioners by using various risk-sharing techniques such as capitation. Spreading the risk to specialists is more difficult because MCOs need specialty care providers in order to make the health care product attractive to purchasers. If specialists are in demand in an area, forcing risk-sharing may lead to nonparticipation by the specialist, or even more damaging, push the specialist onto a competitor's provider panel. As a matter of course, specialists are often reimbursed by a system of UCR fees. In that system, overcharges by specialists can be controlled through the provision that the specialist seek reimbursement from the patient if the fee charges are greater than the contracted fee-for-service.

Another critical component needed by the MCO is an accurate data retrieval system. Such systems can track membership trends, revenues and expenses, or other aspects of the MCO that can affect the profit margin of the organization. Accuracy of data and speed of reporting are key components allowing management to alter trends or take corrective action as needed.

Gatekeepers

As has been indicated, primary care physicians are designated as gatekeepers to patient entry into the health care system created by the MCO. Primary care providers include family practitioners, pediatricians, internists, and gynecologists. These physicians are recruited by the independent practice association (IPA) that contracts to provide services for the MCO's clients or by the MCO itself in the staff model. The function of the gatekeeper is to provide routine health care to the individuals enrolled in the MCO as well as to determine when the individual needs specialist care. The primary care physician is also charged to manage the health care of the individual even in the case where the care is being provided by the specialist. Hence, the primary care physician manages not only the health care of the individual but also manages the access of the individual into the system. Access to specialty care is a critical component, and use of the primary care physician as the gatekeeper raises questions of ethics and quality of patient care. Another important role of the primary care physician is to influence the individual into reducing personal risk of illness or injury through various methods of prevention. Some methods of illness prevention are well-known and their effect on reducing health care costs in general are well documented. Prenatal care, immunizations, smoking cessation, lowering cholesterol, moderate exercise, and mammography have all been proven to lower the cost of health care in various populations. However, these methods require patient compliance, and the primary care physician is in the best position to convince the individual patient of the efficacy of prevention. The MCO can enhance this advocacy by offering incentives through lower copayments or through discounts for out-of-pocket expenses to individual patients. If prevention can truly improve the health status of the client population, then it is in the best interest of the MCO to enforce methods of prevention. Improved health status of the client population means less MCO resources are used for benefit payouts; therefore, the profit margin of the MCO is enhanced.

Cost Reduction Methods

A MCO reduces its costs by spreading the medical benefit expenses into the purchaser, provider, and patient groups. Purchasers are asked to bear some of the risk by the use of deductibles when MCO services are used. The purchaser has the option of passing the deductible on to the individual client (when the purchaser is the employer) or by absorbing the deductible as a fringe benefit. Negotiations by the MCO with purchasers for future contract premiums can be based on previous years' costs. Patient groups are also asked to bear the cost of medical care by requirements for copayments for prescription medications, dollar limits on selected services, restrictions on provider organizations, and deductibles for specific services. But it is at the provider level where the MCO effects its largest cost reductions.

Commonly, MCOs require providers to accept a cap of the reimbursement of fees for services. Capitation occurs when the MCO agrees to pay a provider organization (hospital, IPA, etc) a specific percentage of the premium collected each month for each individual in the service organization's area. If the cost of providing care for the agreed-upon numbers of individuals in the patient population exceeds the allocation of the premium percentage, then the provider organization absorbs the excess cost of care. Individual patient populations are referred to as "lives" (eg, MCO X has an enrollment of 10,000 lives), and the reimbursement rate is based on "per member per month," or PMPM. As seen earlier, PMPM rates can be based on tiers of age, sex, health risk behaviors, family status, and other parameters. Primary care physician reimbursement is capped as a routine matter.

The final method of controlling cost by the MCO is by offering an integrated delivery system (IDS) that ensures the continuum of care. Successful MCOs have integrated all levels of provider organizations into a system that streams the individual into the health or medical organization that can serve the individual patient best at that point of time. Again, through the action of the gatekeeper, an individual is funneled into the most appropriate organizational entity to receive the necessary care. It is conceivable that the patient's wishes would be overridden by the necessity of the gatekeeper adhering to MCO policies. However, since the MCO can contract with the various organizations to provide appropriate care at reduced fees, total health care costs can be lowered.

MCOs can force risk-sharing by providers because of the large number of lives that are enrolled in the MCO. Risk-sharing is seen as advantageous to the MCO since risk can be placed closest to those that actually have some control over medical care costs. Providers accept risk in order to lock in a patient base, maintain local control of health care, and eliminate middlemen who can hold up reimbursements.[9] Providers can also collect monetary awards for successful completion of goals negotiated with the MCO.

Pyenson[9] states that are three elements of risk assumption that providers should be aware of and seek to minimize in their practices. The first element is *underpricing*. Since the use of capitation does not allow for additional funding for claim excess, other than for catastrophic claims, it is important for the provider to be as accurate as possible when setting prices. The second element is *fluctuation*. *Fluctuation* is the unanticipated submission of large-scale claims for medical care. Usually, fluctuation is the result of a natural disaster or massive accident. Providers should negotiate for additional funding for fluctuation, particularly in light of the fact that most MCOs carry reinsurance. The final element of risk assumption by the provider is *common business practices*. The provider needs to negotiate for or otherwise budget for administrative costs. Administrative costs are incurred by the provider in collecting copayments, managing and distributing capitation payments, collecting performance data, and maintaining the managerial staffing necessary to run the organization.

One method of risk assumption has already been discussed. Capitation is commonly used. Other methods used by MCOs to spread the risk include guaranteed discounts by providers off of billed charges, per diem rates for inpatient services, per case rates for all services, and withholds.[10] Withholds are becoming more popular for MCOs. In a withhold, a certain percentage of the premium payment is held by the MCO until the end of the contract period. If there have been additional claims for reimbursement, the amount is subtracted from the withhold and the remainder is returned to the provider. Withholds are often used to provide incentive to the provider to maintain rigorous control over medical care costs.

Provider Accountability

MCOs can demand provider accountability through utilization reviews, outcomes measurements, and emphasis on quality. Utilization reviews are designed to ensure that the type of care proposed by the physician provider is necessary. Techniques include prior approval screens, preadmission certification, second opinions, retrospective chart reviews, and concurrent length of inpatient stay reviews. MCOs also call for outcomes measurements to see that the type of care used for a patient (usually by diagnosis) was effective in relieving the patient's complaints. Outcomes measurements are performed by the provider to show that the care was cost-effective, appropriate for the diagnosis, and appreciated by the patient. Outcomes measurements also have the added appeal to providers of indicating which of several treatment pathways is most effective for any given diagnosis. Finally, the MCO can insist on delivery of quality care by the provider. However, quality of care is defined by the patient and the purchaser rather than by the provider, as had been the case in the past.

Types of Managed Care Organizations

Wagner[11] provides a well-defined differentiation among the four common types of MCOs:
1. HMOs
2. Preferred provider organizations (PPOs)
3. Exclusive provider organizations (EPOs)
4. Point-of-service plans (POS)

HMOs can be seen not only as payers of health care costs but also as providers of health care services. The concept of prepaid health care, wherein a provider was guaranteed a set reimbursement amount by the payer for each member of the plan (regardless of whether the member actually used any services) is a hallmark of HMOs. Because of the synthesis of roles, HMOs are also responsible for ensuring adequate access to providers as well as ensuring the quality of care rendered by contracted providers. There are five models of HMOs that are distinguished from each other by the type of contract used with providers. The first is a staff model in which the HMO directly employs the providers. This model is also known as the closed-panel HMO because only providers hired by the HMO can treat enrollees of the HMO. The second model is the group model. In this model, the HMO contracts with a multispecialty provider group to render care to the enrollees. The provider group is not limited to treating only HMO enrollees and can accept other patients. The third model is the network model. In this case, the HMO contracts with several provider groups across a geographical area to provide services. As in the group model, providers are able to treat other patients besides the HMO enrollees. The fourth model is the individual practice association (IPA) model. In this model, the providers belong to an independent association that negotiates the contract with the HMO. This is an open-panel HMO since the providers are chosen by the IPA, not by the HMO. The last model is the direct contact model. Here, the HMO contracts with an individual provider. This model differs only in scale from the IPA model.

PPOs are organizations of providers that are chosen by purchasers of health care services to provider those services to covered individuals.[11] Characteristics of PPOs include select provider panel (ie, closed); negotiated payment such as discounted, per-diem, diagnosis-related group (DRG), or bundled (all-inclusive cost for a given treatment protocol) rates; rapid payment terms; utilization management; and freedom of consumer choice (individuals are allowed to seek care from non-PPO providers but must pay a larger portion of the cost of treatment). EPOs are quite similar to PPOs in structure but differ in that covered individuals may not seek care from outside providers unless the individuals are willing to pay for the entire cost of treatment themselves. POS plans are a hybrid of HMO and PPO plans.[11] Covered individuals are able to choose at any given time whether they wish to stay inside the PPO for care or utilize non-PPO providers. The major difference with the PPO model lies in reimbursing the provider. In a POS plan, when the covered individual steps outside the PPO panel to receive care, the payment reverts to a fee-for-service method, and the covered individual pays a much larger percentage of the total cost of care. Despite the potential for paying larger amounts out-of-pocket, POS plans are becoming more popular. In 1993, only 7% of employees enrolled in MCO plans were in POS plans. By 1997, POS plans accounted for 20% of MCO enrollees.[7]

TRENDS IN REIMBURSEMENT AND THE FUTURE OF HEALTH CARE

Trying to forecast future changes in reimbursement, especially in rehabilitation, is akin to trying to forecast the end of the world. It is a given that it will happen eventually, but how and by what remains a mystery. If there is a predictor at this time, it seems to be the federal government. It is arguable that the health insurance industry would have inevitably made its way into managed care, but it took the debates over the Clinton health care reform movement to push the industry into revising itself. One can surmise that the combination of large annual increases in health care costs in the 1980s, shrinking profit margins, and the reform movement allowed the health insurance industry the impetus to transform itself before it could be forced into changing by the federal government. In so far as rehabilitation trends go, the federal government is again leading the way in ratcheting down reimbursements. In 1999, the Health Care Financing Administration (HCFA) changed its reimbursement policies for Medicare in two ways. First, HCFA set a $1500 total annual cap for reimbursement of outpatient physical, speech, and hearing therapies.[12] Occupational therapy was excluded from this cap. The cap apparently will be by provider/facility, not by patient, thus allowing the patient to seek appropriate therapy from a different provider/facility when a cap is reached at a specific facility.[12] In 2000, HCFA suspended the cap for reimbursement until 2002. The purpose of the suspension is to allow HCFA to determine a more realistic method of reimbursement for rehabilitation. Second, in skilled nursing facilities, rehabilitation providers are required to track the amount of time spent in each phase of treating a Medicare patient. This will result in the requisite increase in the amount of documentation needed for reimbursement. It is conceivable that private payers will follow the lead of HCFA if it can be determined that these two measures result in comparable patient outcomes at a lower cost.

More daunting than forecasting the future of reimbursement is trying to foreshadow the future of health care. Already, MCOs are seeing the necessity of raising premium prices as their costs rise. Increased state regulation of managed care is becoming common. Laws are being passed that call for HMO or PPO panels to accept any willing provider, that limit the "gag clauses" that prohibit providers from informing patients of treatment protocols that are not covered by the MCO, and that mandate rapid responses to patient appeals of denied services by the MCO. Agreements between physicians and hospitals to form single entities (physician-hospital organizations, or PHOs) that once negotiated contracts with MCOs are increasingly being metamorphosed into integrated delivery systems (IDSs). Kleinke[5] proposes a new set of initials: EHO. In his concept, emerging health care organizations will take the IDS concept into marketing and distribution as well. The EHO will market directly to the purchaser (whether employer or individual) both as a payer of services and as a provider of services. The EHO will manage costs through control of medical supplies, by superior contracting capabilities as the result of enhanced information systems, by limiting bureaucracy and its subsequent costs, by increasing use of all prevention screening and treatment options, and by limited use of heroic measures at the end-stages of life. In his theory, Kleinke[5] states, that in any given geographical area, one or two national EHOs are pitted against one or two local EHOs. The fallout will be between the resources of the national EHOs that can keep premiums lower versus the patient familiarity and comfortableness with the local EHO.

In all likelihood, the dichotomy that exists between the need to hold health care costs as low as possible and the American philosophy of independence of choice for health care providers will continue to influence health care reimbursement in this country for the next century, just as it has for the past century.

REFERENCES

1. Anderson O. *The Health Services Continuum in Democratic States.* Ann Arbor, Mich: AUPHA Press/Health Administration Press; 1989.

3. Enzmann D. *Surviving in Health Care.* St. Louis, Mo: Mosby; 1997.

2. Jost T. *Regulation of the Health Care Professions.* Chicago, Ill: Health Administration Press; 1997.

4. Ward DL. Operational finance and budgeting. In: PR Kongstvedt, ed. *Essentials of Managed Health Care.* Gaithersburg, Md: Aspen Publishers, Inc; 1995.

5. Kleinke JD. *Bleeding Edge.* Gaithersburg, Md: Aspen Publishers, Inc; 1998.

6. Gold MR. Understanding the roots: health maintenance organizations in historical context. In: MR Gold, ed. *Contemporary Managed Care.* Chicago, Ill: Health Administration Press; 1998.

7. Findlay S. *Making sense of a bustling health care market. The state of health care in America 1998.* Frankfurt, Germany: Hoechst Marion Roussel; 1998;8-14.

8. Managed care won't keep health care spending in check. *On Managed Care.* 1998;3(11):1.

9. Pyenson BS. What are managed care risks? In: BS Pyenson, ed. *Calculated Risk.* Chicago, Ill: American Hospital Association Publishing, Inc; 1995.

10. Lee TD. How do providers assume and control risk? In: BS Pyenson, ed. *Calculated Risk.* Chicago, Ill: American Hospital Association Publishing, Inc; 1995.

11. Wagner ER. Types of managed care organizations. In: PR Kongstvedt, ed. *Essentials of Managed Health Care.* Gaithersburg, Md: Aspen Publishers, Inc; 1995.

12. Medicare cap likely to be per provider and likely tracked by facility number; SNFS appear big losers. *Eli's Rehab Report.* 1998;5(19):178.

Chapter Two

Athletic Training and Third-Party Reimbursement

OBJECTIVES

Following the completion of this chapter, the reader will be able to:
- Trace the history of reimbursement for certified athletic trainers.
- Define the mission statement of the National Athletic Trainers' Association (NATA).
- Identify the importance of reimbursement for certified athletic trainers.
- Identify the existing challenges related to achieving reimbursement.
- Recognize and understand the effect of Medicare recognition of certified athletic trainers.
- Define current procedural terminology (CPT) codes and understand their use in billing.

HISTORY

The NATA was formally organized in 1950. Since that time, its professional member the NATA Board of Certification (NATABOC) certified athletic trainer has been providing health care services to individuals participating in formally organized athletic programs. Certified athletic trainers have historically been employed by college/university athletic departments, professional sport organizations, and more recently, secondary school corporations to provide health and injury care to the athletes under their jurisdiction.

In the early 1980s, certified athletic trainers ventured into the sports medicine clinic arena, providing health care to a variety of physically active populations, primarily recreational sports participants. In addition, they began providing clinic-sponsored athletic training outreach services to secondary school athletic departments. In 1990, the American Medical Association (AMA) and its Council on Medical Education formally recognized athletic training as an allied health profession, creating a professional identity for athletic trainers in the health care community.

In 1992, the NATA Board of Directors revised the mission statement of the NATA to reflect the broad categories of patient populations served by athletic trainers. The current mission statement of the NATA is, "to enhance the quality of health care for athletes and those engaged in physical activity and to advance the profession of athletic training through education and research in the prevention, evaluation, management, and rehabilitation of injuries" (as ruled by the NATA Board of Directors, 1999). This statement clearly reflects the philosophy of the versatility of today's certified athletic trainer in the health care marketplace.

As athletic trainers became integrated into the private, corporate, and hospital-based sports medicine clinic settings, economic health care issues such as third-party reimbursement became extremely relevant. It became apparent that professional identity, recognition, and job opportunity and stability were going to be directly dependent on the identification and recognition of the certified athletic trainer as a reimbursable entity.

In 2000, NATA membership statistics reflected that approximately 40% of certified athletic trainers were employed by sports medicine clinics, 26% by colleges/universities, and 25% by secondary schools. A small percentage worked in industrial settings and with professional sport teams. Employment opportunities continue to diversify for athletic trainers and have expanded to the industrial workplace. Athletic trainers have become providers of injury prevention and rehabilitation services to industrial employees working on assembly lines and in factory settings. The same skills that have made certified athletic trainers extremely effective in providing health and injury care to athletes are now being recognized by physically active people of all ages in a variety of settings.

THE IMPORTANCE OF REIMBURSEMENT

To establish and maintain a valued and respected position in the health care marketplace, it is imperative that the certified athletic trainer become a reimbursable entity. Employers in the clinical setting have difficulty justifying hiring nonreimbursable health care providers when other reimbursable professionals are available. It is becoming increasingly difficult from an economic perspective for employers in sports medicine clinics to justify hiring athletic trainers for outreach programs to area athletic teams. The marketing value of this practice is difficult to measure and substantiate. Patient referrals are no longer guaranteed due to payer restrictions. Physician choices are determined by payers, no longer by individual preference and choice.

Health care costs related to care of college and university athletes continue to increase, as does the cost of providing allied health care personnel to provide care for this population and maintain the necessary paperwork and documentation required by payers. Because of this, traditional athletic training settings (eg, college and university athletic departments) are exploring ways to maximize economic efficiency by creating and developing profit centers within their sports medicine departments. Utilizing reimbursable health care providers is essential to the business plan associated with these programs. Furthermore, obtaining reimbursement for athletic trainers protects jobs in the traditional setting by preventing the influx of employment of reimbursable providers, an attractive revenue-producing option for athletic departments.

Administrators and athletic trainers in the secondary school settings are also pursuing ways to apply the principles of reimbursement to the medical services provided to their interscholastic athletes. Billing athletes' insurance for soft goods (eg, braces and supports) as well as postsurgical rehabilitation performed by the schools' athletic trainers may become commonplace in the future, but only if athletic trainers are reimbursable.

To maintain and secure employment opportunities in the health care arena regardless of practice setting, it is apparent that the certified athletic trainer must become a recognized reimbursable entity. Other allied health care professions have evolved to this status and providers in a variety of specialties (eg, physical therapy, occupational therapy, speech therapy, and others) receive third-party reimbursement for the services that they provide. Other evolving professions, such as kinesiotherapists, medical specialty physician assistants, massage therapists, and providers of complementary therapies, are seeking this status as well. As competition for a very limited health care dollar increases, it is necessary that certified athletic trainers become recognized as equals among allied health care providers and achieve comparable reimbursement status. The care provided by athletic trainers must be valued by patients and clients, other health care providers, and, most importantly, by payers.

THE NONPHYSICIAN PROVIDER

The process of reimbursement for the delivery of health care services to the physically active is designed in such a way that makes the athletic trainer a valued, effective provider in today's health care system. The health care system in the United States has evolved to a managed care model. Athletic trainers have historically provided services in a managed care fashion. The educational competencies on which the practice of athletic training is based represent an entire continuum of care, including prevention, recognition, treatment, and rehabilitation emphasizing a return to precondition functional levels. The historically evidenced strong working relationship between athletic trainers and physicians illustrates the effective role that athletic trainers play as competent and valued physician extenders and case managers. Providing quality care in a cost-efficient manner describes the role and function of the athletic trainer.

Positioning the certified athletic trainer in the role of nonphysician provider or physician extender most accurately represents the skills that athletic trainers possess. Providing fee-for-service therapy is certainly an important function of certified athletic trainers, but more important is their ability to provide under the direction of a physician initial assessment and case manage individuals' health and injury care. This is the role that best suits certified athletic trainers and the model that must be emphasized.

ACHIEVING REIMBURSEMENT—THE CHALLENGES

A number of challenges exist for the athletic trainer seeking reimbursement. Successful reimbursement efforts are directly linked to individual state athletic training practice acts, defining the legal scope of practice for certified athletic trainers. Currently, approximately 41 states have specific regulatory acts governing the practice of athletic training. The type of regulation, scope of practice, and specific defining language in those acts varies greatly from state to state. Some practice acts limit care provided by athletic trainers to a strictly defined athletic population only, while others are all-inclusive, extending services to the "physically active."

These regulatory differences make it very difficult for athletic trainers to gain nationwide payer recognition. Those states that have restrictive language inhibit the efforts of athletic trainers to be recognized as providers for nontraditional athletic populations. Those states without regulatory acts have difficulty clearly defining the practice of athletic training to payers and other providers and have no legal basis to refer to for their professional practice standards. Efforts continue to establish state licensure for athletic trainers in all 50 states, creating practice acts that incorporate consistent language that clearly defines the broad scope of athletic training practice.

MEDICARE RECOGNITION

Recognition by prominent national payers is the goal of the reimbursement efforts of the NATA. This will provide the greatest impact on individual state efforts and will provide a tremendous impetus to payer relationships throughout the country. There is no more visible or influential national payer than the Health Care Financing Administration's (HCFA's) Medicare/Medicaid program. To be identified as a Medicare-approved provider creates immediate reimbursement recognition among all payers. In addition, a Medicare-approved provider is assigned a provider number, easily facilitating the claims filing process for reimbursement. Although athletic trainers have not historically treated Medicare patients (age 65 and older) and often do not have the skills needed to manage many of the health-related problems associated with this age group, recognition by Medicare establishes an immediate identity for all payers and, with the resultant provider number, would facilitate the reimbursement process for athletic trainers nationwide. Athletic trainers also are not typically exposed to a large Medicaid population (ie, those individuals needing government subsidy to pay for their medical care) and therefore have difficulty demonstrating effectiveness with that population.

Currently, certified athletic trainers are not included as recognized providers in Medicare statutes. HCFA does not recognize athletic training services as reimbursable. A change in the language of Medicare statutes requires US congressional action. Amending the statutes to include additional health care providers is an arduous process. A strong case must be developed and presented justifying the need for additional providers and, more specifically, how the addition will improve, both in effectiveness and economically, the care already available to the Medicare population. Objective evidence must be presented that documents successful health care management with this population and a desire of this population to utilize the services of these new proposed providers.

DOCUMENTING SUCCESS

It is difficult to document successful provider outcomes with a population that is not commonly treated by athletic trainers. Although there are some practice settings employing athletic trainers that have a Medicare patient population, the treatment provided to these patients is typically managed by currently approved Medicare providers. Without a Medicare provider number, it is difficult for employers to utilize athletic trainers in the treatment of these patients. Although within legal boundaries, there is also hesitancy on the part of employers in Medicare-approved facilities to use non-Medicare recognized providers in the treatment of any population fearing implications of Medicare fraud.

An independent legal firm with experience in Medicare law provided the opinion that there is nothing in Medicare law that prohibits certified athletic trainers from providing outpatient rehabilitation services to commercial patients in Medicare-certified outpatient rehabilitation clinics or comprehensive outpatient rehabilitation facilities (CORFs) (Shaw-Pittman Attorneys at Law, Washington, DC, November, 1999).

Demonstration projects designed to document and illustrate the effectiveness of new approaches to traditional health care are a common method of acquiring information and illustrating a need for health care provisions not currently included in existing coverage. These projects are typically regionally organized multicenter research trials lasting 6 months to 1 year, enlisting a patient population large enough to demonstrate statistical significance in data analyses. Demonstration projects are usually conducted at the expense of the group seeking the data to illustrate its case (eg, the athletic training profession). Demonstration projects focused on evaluating the effectiveness of athletic training services provided to a Medicare population could be designed and undertaken.

However, even with positive results, demonstration projects do not guarantee a statute change. They just provide additional supporting documentation for proposed statute amendments. Realistically, proposed statute changes to include additional allied health care providers are likely to be met with great opposition from currently approved Medicare providers of similar services. The extremely competitive health care market and the shrinking reimbursement dollar for rehabilitation services will cause strong lobbying efforts by competitors of athletic training to block Medicare recognition in an effort to protect their employment arenas.

THE VALUE OF PREVENTION

Demonstrating the effective, unique aspects of the practice of athletic training and differentiating the athletic trainer from other allied health care professionals is essential to gaining payer recognition at the national level. Unfortunately, the area of prevention, traditionally a strong skill set for athletic trainers, has not been recognized as a high priority for health care reimbursement. In addition, the current philosophy of recognizing and valuing achieving and maintaining functional levels beyond activities of daily living has not been recognized as a high priority by Congress and the current government administration. Therefore, HCFA does not place a high priority on these health-related quality of life benefits. Private payers and large health maintenance organizations (HMOs) typically follow the philosophies of the government payers.

It is predicted that in the future, however, the US Congress may be forced to re-evaluate its position regarding the value of preventive health care and the demand from the public for high standards of health-related quality of life due to the strong influence of the "baby boomer" population. These health care initiatives may therefore become a priority and, if so, the value of the services provided by athletic trainers will increase dramatically. Until then, it is necessary to continue to educate national payers as to the value of athletic trainers and to lobby for recognition and reimbursement for athletic trainers for traditionally reimbursed health care services.

EFFECTING CHANGE

Efforts to formally lobby the federal government to amend current congressional standards are extremely costly and are met with many obstacles. Full-time lobbyists must be employed to effectively facilitate these changes. However, it is first necessary to build a strong case with objective documentation illustrating the effectiveness and efficiency of care provided by athletic trainers before undertaking specific lobbying action at the national level.

In order to enhance the reimbursement position of the athletic trainer at the national level, continued evidence of reimbursement in all practice settings throughout the United States must continue to be encouraged and documented. Often times, this evidence in and of itself makes a strong statement. Representation of the athletic training profession on various national health care committees is essential and is being pursued.

CURRENT PROCEDURAL TERMINOLOGY CODES

The AMA's Department of Coding and Nomenclature and its current procedural terminology (CPT) Editorial Panel is the group that develops CPT codes, or current procedural terminology, for the purpose of defining those treatments and services provided by health care practitioners. In a 1996 ruling, the AMA specifically clarified that the term "provider" as used in the codes is a general term used to define the individual providing the service described in the code. The provider can be anyone who is licensed to perform the service. In addition, the AMA clarified that the term "therapist" as used in the codes is not intended to denote any specific practice or specialty field. Determination of payment policy in relation to various providers is made by the third-party payer.

That clarification was extremely significant for athletic training reimbursement efforts as it made it possible for certified athletic trainers to utilize appropriate CPT codes for billing purposes as long as they practice in compliance with their state athletic training regulatory act. However, payer recognition of the certified athletic trainer as a reimbursable provider still presents significant challenges. Although CPT codes may be utilized by certified athletic trainers for billing purposes, payers may still deny reimbursement because they are unfamiliar with certified athletic trainers as providers.

In May 2000, the CPT Editorial Panel added two new codes for Athletic Training Evaluation and Athletic Training Reevaluation. This action created a specific identity for athletic trainers in the health care community and dispelled confusion as to who was actually providing the services. The new codes become effective in 2002. Prior to that time, procedure code 97799, unlisted physical medicine/rehabilitation service, should be used.

CPT codes are devised and edited by a panel of physicians and allied health personnel. It is critical that the athletic training profession be represented on CPT panels to address these issues and effect change for the future. Athletic trainers need direct input on CPT coding issues to successfully accomplish widespread reimbursement.

UNIFORM BILLING CODES

Similar to CPT codes, uniform billing (UB) codes are facility codes utilized by hospitals to bill for health care services. These codes are established by a national UB Coding Committee of the American Hospital Association. Changes to these codes or the creation of new codes for additional services is accomplished through amendments proposed to the UB Coding Committee. In November 1999, the UB Coding Committee acted on an official application submitted by the NATA requesting the establishment of a specific code for athletic training services. The committee approved the request by expanding an existing category to include "other therapeutic services" and specifically identified athletic training services as subcategory number one. As a result, effective October 1, 2000, certified athletic trainers working in the hospital setting may utilize UB code 951, which designates athletic training services.

REGULATORY TERMS

Typical language in regulatory codes refers to authorized providers as anyone licensed to perform the specific service(s) described. Following a request for clarification, the AMA CPT Editorial and Information Services offices clarified that the term "licensed" is intended to encompass any designation that a particular state has for regulating health providers. "Licensure," "certification," and "registration" are terms used by different states. The CPT codes may be used by state licensed, state certified, or state registered professionals who have the described service in their state determined to be within their scope of practice.

HEALTH CARE PRACTITIONER ADVISORY COUNCIL

The Health Care Practitioner Advisory Council (HCPAC) of the National Committee for Quality Assurance (NCQA) was established to facilitate better communication between practitioners and the NCQA. The mission of the NCQA is to improve health care in the United States by providing information about the quality of care and service delivered by managed health care systems, which changes how Americans choose their health care and how systems provide it. The NCQA is the watchdog of managed health care systems, including its physician providers. The HCPAC was established to represent nonphysician providers.

The HCPAC is made up of representatives from nonphysician health care professions, giving those groups a vehicle by which to monitor their effectiveness and identify their position in today's managed care health care environment. All major allied health care professions, including the NATA, are seeking HCPAC membership.

PAYER RECOGNITION

The recognition of certified athletic trainers as reimbursable entities by major payers is critical to achieving successful reimbursement. Meetings have taken place with selected major national payers to lobby for the inclusion of certified athletic trainers as recognized providers in their plans. Decisions on provider recognition and inclusion are often made at the state and/or regional levels. Therefore, approaches to payers at these levels is critical to provider recognition.

SUMMARY

As athletic training practice settings diversified, the need for athletic trainers to become recognized as valued, reimbursable providers by the health care community increased dramatically. Athletic training and third-party reimbursement is directly dependent upon recognition of the certified athletic trainer by major payers and representation of athletic trainers on decision-making committees of health care regulatory agencies.

RESOURCES

1. National Athletic Trainers' Association, Inc, 2952 Stemmons Freeway, Dallas, Tex.
2. National Committee for Quality Assurance, 2000 L St, NW, Suite 500, Washington, DC.

Chapter Three

The National Athletic Trainers' Association Reimbursement Advisory Group

OBJECTIVES

Following the completion of this chapter, the reader will be able to:
- Identify the formation and structure of the National Athletic Trainers' Association (NATA) Reimbursement Advisory Group (RAG).
- Define the objectives of the NATA RAG.
- Define outcomes research.
- Describe the Athletic Training Outcomes Assessment (ATOA) study.
- Identify the results of the ATOA study.
- Identify specific reimbursement initiatives and strategies developed and pursued by the NATA RAG.

HISTORY

In 1994, the NATA Board of Directors unanimously resolved to adopt the following position statement in regard to reimbursement for athletic training services: "Athletic trainers may, consistent with governing laws, regulations, and policies, provide appropriate athletic training services on a fee-for-use basis. Athletic trainers will use reasonable and customary fee structures for services reimbursed by private pay patients or third-party payers." In addition, the board unanimously resolved to direct President Denny Miller to speak to the NATA Governmental Affairs Committee and ask to undertake the important project of working on the state level with insurance companies and third-party reimbursement and finding ways to pursue outcomes research.

As a result of those actions, the NATA Board of Directors formed the RAG to study and explore issues relating to athletic trainers and third-party reimbursement. Organizationally, this group was structured to interact with the existing NATA Governmental Affairs Committee and report directly to the NATA Board of Directors. RAG members, representing various practice settings with experience in issues related to governmental affairs, reimbursement, and outcomes research, were appointed by the NATA Board of Directors.

ORIGINAL MEMBERS OF THE REIMBURSEMENT ADVISORY GROUP

- Marjorie J. Albohm, MS, ATC
- Earl Anderson, ATC
- Ronnie Barnes, MS, ATC
- Dan Campbell, ATC, PT
- Martin R. Daniel, ATC
- Pat Forbis, ATC
- Joe J. Godek, MS, ATC
- Bob Gray, MS, ATC
- Tom Koto, ATC
- Steve Tollefson, MS, PT, ATC,
- Keith Webster, MA, ATC
- Stephen E. Bair, ATC, NATA Board of Directors Liaison

GROUP OBJECTIVES

The RAG defined three initial objectives:
1. Create a model approach to prospective payers.
2. Develop and implement a nationwide outcomes study to assess care provided by certified athletic trainers.
3. Educate the NATA members and its constituents on issues relating to third-party reimbursement

The overall goal was to create a model to follow for those certified athletic trainers choosing to pursue third-party reimbursement in their practice setting and to provide the tools necessary to successfully pursue that goal. The group emphasized the role of the athletic trainer as a recognized health care provider and physician extender rather than that of an assistant or aide to other allied health care providers.

APPROACH TO PAYERS

In pursuit of the first objective, a packet of information was developed for use by certified athletic trainers pursuing third-party reimbursement. The packet was subsequently revised in 2000. The informational packet includes an overall guide to reimbursement and approaching payers (see Appendix 1). Also included in the packet are Medicare, current procedural terminology (CPT) code, and uniform billing (UB) code information and related interpretations (see Appendix 2). In addition, information from the American Medical Association (AMA) recognizing and supporting the role of athletic trainers as health care providers, educational standards and competencies on which the profession is based, background information on the profession of athletic training and its professional organization, NATA Board of Certification standards and continuing education requirements (see Appendix 3), and results of the NATA nationwide outcomes study are included (see Appendix 4).

This packet of information is available to state athletic training association presidents and state reimbursement committees for appropriate use and dissemination. An emphasis was placed on developing individual state reimbursement advisory committees that would plan appropriate organized approaches to reimbursement within each state. Due to the differences in athletic training state regulatory acts, it is difficult to develop a national plan that would be appropriate for each state. Emphasis was placed on an organized approach through the state associations, rather than an individual approach, with individual entities seeking reimbursement from a multitude of payers. Each state president and/or reimbursement chairperson is asked to communicate directly to members of the NATA RAG regarding the details and progress of their reimbursement activities. Currently, approximately 30 states have organized RAGs within their state athletic training associations. Other states' associations have designated specific individuals as reimbursement contacts.

OUTCOMES RESEARCH

Health care reform gave significant impetus to the development of medical effectiveness research commonly known as outcomes research. Health care standards require the identification and determination of effective and necessary interventions that significantly improve the function and quality of life of patients.[1,2] Patient outcomes assessment can be defined as the collection of any information that demonstrates the effect of health care interventions on the health status of patients.[2-5] Outcomes assessment is a technology of patient experience designed to document changes in a patient's clinical condition. Outcomes has also been defined as a change in physical function that is meaningful to the patient and is related to services provided.[6,7] It is designed to measure patients' functional status and quality of life over time using terms relevant to patients, providers, and purchasers.

Allied health care professionals have become increasingly involved in determining whether the care they provide effects change. The current health care climate of assessment and accountability is the driving force behind the emphasis on this determination.[1] This era of assessment and accountability evolved from a need for cost containment, a renewed sense of competition, and the results of successful outcomes studies. Quality assessment is the measurement of the technical and interpersonal aspects of medical care.[7] Quality of care affects clinical outcomes, functional outcomes, and patient satisfaction.[8] With the emphasis on cost containment, quality of care becomes an issue of major concern for patients, providers, and payers.

Traditionally, health care has been assessed in many ways, including assessments of structure, process, and outcome, all of which are distinguishably different.[9] It is suggested that judging health care by its outcome is more appropriate than judging it by structure or process.[9] Outcomes research measures the effect of the health care process. When addressing outcomes, the patient's perception is of paramount importance. Their goals and expectations must be addressed. Outcomes analyses is useful in benchmarking standards and identifying relationships between quality of care and patients' value systems.[8] Outcomes research, by assessing the benefit of therapeutic intervention, is therefore essential for accountability among health care practitioners (Tables 3-1 and 3-2).[9,10]

Outcomes can be valuable and beneficial in relation to patient outcome, provider comparisons, facility comparisons, quality assurance, and cost/benefits analyses. Table 3-3 states the benefits of outcomes analyses. Outcomes research analyses can benefit patients, providers, and payers, as well as contribute to the scientific research body of knowledge.

Table 3-1

Outcomes Research Is Designed to Answer Six Basic Questions

1. Is treatment provided better than no treatment?
2. Is treatment worse than no treatment?
3. Is one treatment better than another?
4. If a treatment is effective, is a little just as good as a lot?
5. Does quality of life change because condition has changed?
6. Are the benefits of treatment worth the cost?

Table 3-2

Value of Outcomes Data

- Identify problem areas requiring further investigation.
- Better align goals and objectives with client needs.
- Availability of data for research purposes.
- Ability to determine cost-benefit analysis.
- Develop practice guidelines, treatment protocols.
- Develop consensus statements.
- Validate effectiveness, efficiency.
- Enhance payer relationships.

OUTCOMES AND THE CERTIFIED ATHLETIC TRAINER

Data validating the certified athletic trainer as an effective and efficient health care practitioner were nonexistent. Therefore, the RAG decided to develop and implement a nationwide outcomes research study demonstrating the outcome of care provided by certified athletic trainers in a variety of practice settings.

In the early summer of 1995, a request for proposal (RFP) seeking potential investigators to design and conduct an athletic training outcomes study was published. A RAG subcommittee screened the proposals and selected three for further consideration. Individual interviews were conducted and the project was awarded to Lyle Knudson, EdD, of Bio*Analysis Systems, Inc., Frisco, Colo. The NATA Board of Directors allocated $150,000 to conduct the outcomes study over a 3-year period. This financial commitment distinguished the NATA as the first allied health care professional association to fund an outcomes study for its professional members.

> ### Table 3-3
> ### BENEFITS OF OUTCOMES ANALYSES
>
> - Identification of problem areas requiring more investigation.
> - Better alignment of goals and objectives with client needs.
> - Availability of data for research purposes.
> - Information on cost-effectiveness.

The outcomes subcommittee of the RAG worked with Bio*Analysis Systems, Inc to further define the study methodology, instrumentation, data collection procedures, analyses, and associated timelines. A pilot study was conducted in the fall of 1995. Data collection site selection began and continued through January 1996. The study officially commenced January 1, 1996, and data collection was completed December 31, 1998.

ATHLETIC TRAINING OUTCOMES ASSESSMENT

The ATOA was developed for the NATA by Bio*Analysis Systems. A customized, validated outcomes data collection instrument was developed to assess patient status pre- and post-treatment by certified athletic trainers. The completed outcomes assessment study includes data on 5506 patients at 125 data collection sites throughout the United States during the period between January 1, 1996 and December 31, 1998 on patients with physician-diagnosed musculoskeletal injury. Data collection sites reflect all settings where certified athletic trainers are employed. These include colleges/universities, secondary schools, sports medicine clinics, sports medicine clinic outreach, professional sports, and industrial settings. Single credentialed certified athletic trainers were the required providers. It was required that they provided 90% of the patient care, including pre- and post-treatment evaluation.

ATOA outcomes are defined in terms of patient improvements in various individual and grouped factors between pre- and post-treatment evaluations, as rated on a 0 to 4 scale by each patient and respective athletic trainer. The individual and grouped factors include functional outcomes (activities of daily living, work activities, sport/recreation/wellness activities), physical outcomes (movement capacity, strength/power capacity, endurance, motor abilities, body structure impairment, and sensory), general health status, specific medical condition, and psychosocial status. The overall outcome is a compilation of all individual factors. In addition, at discharge, patients rated their satisfaction with the treatment services and the athletic trainer. The athletic trainer rated patient compliance and coach/supervisor's cooperation with the treatment.

OUTCOMES RESULTS

Analysis of the data reveals a very positive impression by patients regarding the care provided by certified athletic trainers. The outcomes are consistent across site types. Using a scale of 0 = lowest rating and 4 = highest rating, important findings are:[13]
- Participants (5506 patients) rated their satisfaction with certified athletic trainers at 3.89.
- Patients rated their overall pretreatment status at 2.40. Following a treatment program by a certified athletic trainer, patients rated their overall status at 3.57.

- Patients' ratings of their overall status prior to treatment by certified athletic trainers were 2.24 in sports medicine clinics (2307 patients), 2.48 in high schools (919 athletes), 2.62 in colleges and universities (929 athletes), and 2.44 in industrial settings (1110 workers). These values increased to 3.41 in sports medicine clinics, 3.75 in high schools, 3.71 in colleges and universities, and 3.61 in industrial settings following the completion of treatment programs by certified athletic trainers.
- Participants (5506 patients) rated their pretreatment ability to participate in sports or recreational activities at 1.75. Upon discharge from a program of care provided by the certified athletic trainer, patients rated their ability to participate in sports or recreational activities at 3.31.
- Participants (5506 patients) rated their pretreatment ability to participate in work-related activities at 2.15. Following a treatment program by a certified athletic trainer, the rating increased to 3.48.
- Prior to initiating a program of care provided by a certified athletic trainer following injury or surgery, 5506 patients rated their status for movement, strength, and sensory perceptions at 2.18, 2.19, and 2.09, respectively. Upon discharge, patients rated their values at 3.57, 3.50, and 3.47, respectively.
- Participants (403 patients) who underwent reconstructive surgery rated their overall status at the initiation of treatment by the certified athletic trainer at 2.00. At discharge from the treatment program, the patients rated their overall status at 3.47.
- Participants (158 patients) with grade III, or severe, sprains rated their overall status at 2.03 at the initiation of treatment by a certified athletic trainer. The rating improved to a value of 3.44 at discharge from the treatment program.
- The average number of treatments provided during the treatment program ranged from a high of 18.84 for colleges and universities to a low of 12.18 in sports medicine clinic settings. The average for industrial settings and high schools were 13.20 and 14.25, respectively.
- The total number of treatments provided is a positive factor in determining overall outcomes.
- As the number of days increased between the date of injury or surgery and the beginning of treatments by the certified athletic trainer, the patients' rating of their overall outcomes decreased.

Additionally, athletic training methods produce excellent overall outcomes with the best results in functional outcomes (particularly in sport, recreation, wellness, and work activities), and in physical outcomes (eg, movement—range of motion, sensory—pain relief). Athletic training is effective in treating injuries at all body locations, especially in lower extremities and the cervicothoracolumbar spine.

The most effective athletic training modalities, among those frequently used, appear to be cold packs, ice massage, heat packs, therapeutic exercise, functional activity exercises, electrotherapy, and taping/bracing. Work hardening appears to by very effective with industrial patients. Athletic training outcomes are fairly consistent across site types, referring sources, and payer groups.

Clearly, the outcomes study demonstrates that care provided by certified athletic trainers effects change, and patients value the care they receive from certified athletic trainers. These outcomes data provide objective validation of care provided by certified athletic trainers and can be used to demonstrate value to payers.

OUTCOMES STUDY PUBLICATIONS

Results of the athletic training outcomes study were published in 1999 in a manuscript titled "An Outcomes Assessment of Care Provided by Certified Athletic Trainers" by Albohm and Wilkerson.[11] The NATA Research and Education Foundation published a request for proposals (RFP) for outcomes studies (see Appendix 5), providing access to the NATA outcomes database for additional scientific inquiry leading to manuscript preparation.

COMPARATIVE ANALYSES

Additional analyses of outcomes data addressing specific points of inquiry and specific comparisons will continue. In addition to the Bio*Analysis national database, Focus on Therapeutic Outcomes, Inc (FOTO, Inc) provides outcomes services for contracted clients. FOTO, Inc maintains a national database for a variety of health care professions.

In 1999, the NATA RAG commissioned FOTO, Inc to conduct a comparative analysis of care provided by certified athletic trainers and physical therapists in a clinical setting. Results of that analysis indicated that certified athletic trainers provide the same levels of outcomes, value, and patient satisfaction as physical therapists in a clinical setting.[12]

EDUCATION

The third objective of the RAG was to educate the NATA membership and its constituencies on issues related to reimbursement, including the effect of health care reform and the evolution of managed care within our health care system on athletic training. Athletic trainers traditionally have not been exposed to the traditional health care system and, therefore, do not have a great deal of experience in dealing with third-party payer issues. Members from the RAG began to attend each NATA district meeting making presentations regarding reimbursement issues. Monthly articles relating to reimbursement began being published in the *NATA News*. Three-hour symposia were presented at each NATA annual meeting. In addition, special articles on key issues associated with athletic trainers and reimbursement were prepared and disseminated on an as-needed basis. A reimbursement resource center was established within the department of governmental affairs at the NATA office.

STUDY STATES

Once the initial objectives of the RAG were defined, work began on developing the specific aspects of those objectives. Five states were chosen as study states for reimbursement efforts and to explore issues related to reimbursement. It was hopeful that this exploration would create guidelines and models for other states to follow.

The states included Massachusetts, Ohio, Indiana, Illinois, and Washington. These states were selected because of the flexibility of their athletic training regulatory acts allowing certified athletic trainers to manage the health care of physically active people rather than just athletes. Washington was selected because it is an unregulated state and therefore would allow exploration of reimbursement opportunities in states where no athletic training regulatory act exists.

Each study state identified a group of leaders within its state athletic training association to consult on reimbursement issues. NATA legal council and individual state lobbyists worked together to study each state regulatory act in an effort to understand the scope of practice for athletic trainers in each state. A conference call was held with state association representatives and RAG representatives to determine specific strategies to pursue regarding approaches to specific payers.

The variety of experiences gained from these state-specific efforts were shared with members and used as guidelines for other states' reimbursement efforts. The overall opinion following this analysis led to the conclusion that reimbursement was very state-specific based on individual athletic training practice acts and quite varied within each state based on payer reimbursement patterns.

In working with individual state associations to pursue reimbursement, an attempt was made to insert specific reimbursement language in proposed athletic training legislation. Specific language included mandating reimbursement for athletic training services and prohibiting the denial of reimbursement for services provided by certified athletic trainers. This approach was attempted in a number of states without success due to strong opposition by other allied health care professions and by payers. The language was ultimately deleted from the proposed legislation before it reached final vote. As a result, this approach was abandoned.

However, in 1999, landmark legislation was passed in Georgia, including language related to athletic training reimbursement.[13] This legislation became the model for other states to follow.

The experience gained from working with state associations further reinforced the RAG's philosophy of creating a unified approach to reimbursement within each state based on the specific athletic training legislation defining the legal scope of practice for athletic trainers.

REIMBURSEMENT CONSULTANTS

To assist in understanding the intricacies of health care reform and the American health care system, a managed care consultant was retained to work with the RAG on positioning athletic trainer as health care providers in the evolving managed care health care system. This consultant, Polly Rhenwall, Health Care Business Development Specialist (Atlanta, Ga) worked with the RAG in developing specific initiatives directed at managed care organizations. Large national managed care payers were identified and specific approaches were developed for these groups. It was soon realized that it would be very difficult to gain the attention of managed care groups since the dollars spent on rehabilitation were so limited and prevention was not considered a valuable commodity. Information regarding managed care was disseminated to the NATA members, and Ms. Rhenwall's consulting services remain available for future managed care strategies.

Recognition and identification as an approved provider by the Health Care Finance Administration (HCFA), the government entity that oversees Medicare and Medicaid, represents the gold standard in health care reimbursement. In an effort to achieve this recognition for athletic trainers, a Medicare consultant was hired to develop a plan of approach to HCFA with the goal to have certified athletic trainers included in the Medicare statutes as approved Medicare providers. The Medicare consultant Mary Ellen George, Medicare Survey Specialist (Plymouth, Mass) worked with a subcommittee of the RAG to develop a plan of approach to HCFA. A face-to-face meeting with representatives from HCFA's Coverage and Analysis Group in the Office of Standards and Quality subsequently occurred. Through that meeting it was learned that formal congressional action was needed to amend Medicare statutes to add approved providers. It was the feeling of the HCFA representatives that this was possible to achieve since other allied health care professions have been added in the past, but significant lobbying efforts would be needed and a change in thinking among the current legislature regarding the value of prevention and health-related quality of life issues would need to occur to accomplish this goal. The HCFA representatives encouraged further documentation regarding the effectiveness of care provided by athletic trainers and documentation of athletic training reimbursement by payers throughout the country.

REIMBURSEMENT STRATEGIES

In January 1998, the RAG developed reimbursement strategies for NATA members. These strategies provided further organized reimbursement efforts and group consultants to members pursuing reimbursement. The strategies are as follows:

I. Approach to payers
   A. District, state levels
      1. RAG committee consultants are assigned by district to assist individual state efforts within each district with reimbursement efforts (Table 3-4).
         - Individual state presidents, state reimbursement representatives, and/or district directors are encouraged to contact assigned committee members for assistance.
         - Emphasis should be on approaching insurance companies who have demonstrated evidence of recognizing athletic trainers as reimbursable entities in other states (eg, Prudential, Blue Cross/Blue Shield).
   B. Specific settings
      1. RAG committee consultants are identified by practice expertise (Table 3-5).
         - Individual state presidents, state reimbursement representatives, and/or district directors are encouraged to contact these individuals to assist with reimbursement efforts in those designated specific practice settings.
   C. National level
      1. To assist with national efforts directed at amending Medicare statutes, members are encouraged to identify their national legislators and establish direct communication with them regarding the importance of this issue.
         - Identification of legislators can be obtained by contacting the NATA manager of governmental relations.
         - RAG committee consultants are available to assist with these efforts and assist in developing specific strategies for approaches.
         - NATA legal counsel is available to assist with appointments with legislators in Washington and has offered to accompany members on appointments with legislators when in Washington.

GOALS REDEFINED

In June 1998, the RAG met to assess its progress in achieving its goals over the previous 3 years. It was decided that many of the original goals of the group had been met and a redefinition of goals needed to take place. The RAG concluded that reimbursement continued to be a critical issue for the profession of athletic training. An increasing number of certified athletic trainers are being affected by reimbursement issues; therefore, the need to pursue reimbursement continues to grow. The RAG revised its mission and goals to ensure continued dialogue and progress on this extremely critical issue. Following is the revised mission and goals of the NATA RAG.

Mission: *To enhance the reimbursement interests and efforts of NATABOC certified athletic   trainers.*
Goals:
1. *Continue to educate NATA members about reimbursement issues.*
2. *Encourage the establishment of reimbursement committees within each state athletic training association.*

Table 3-4

1998 REIMBURSEMENT ADVISORY GROUP COMMITTEE CONSULTANTS

Districts I and II

Jeff Konin, ATC, MPT
Delaware Tech Community College
Owens Campus
Georgetown, DE 19947
302-856-5400
302-856-5773 (fax)

District III

Keith J. Webster, MA, ATC
EJ Nutter Training Facility
Room 136
Sports Center Dr.
606-257-6521
606-257-8953 (fax)

District IV

Dan Campbell, ATC, PT
Gunderson Lutheran Sports Medicine Center
3100 S. Kinney Coulee Rd.
Onalaska, WI 54650
608-796-8610
608-796-8614 (fax)

Districts V and VI

Pat Forbis, ATC
Capitol Region Sports Medicine & Rehabilitation

1500 B SW Blvd.
Jefferson City, MO 65109
573-761-4131
573-761-4221 (fax)

District VII

Marjorie J. Albohm, MS, ATC
The Center for Hip and Knee Surgery
1199 Hadley Rd.
Mooresville, IN 46158
317-831-2273
317-831-9347 (fax)

Districts VIII and X

Steve Tollefson, PT, ATC, MS
14511 183rd Ave. NE
Woodinville, WA 98072
206-481-0494
206-481-6221 (fax)

District IX

Jay Shoop, ATC
Georgia Institute of Technology
150 Bobby Dodd Way
Atlanta, GA 30332
404-894-5461
404-894-1524 (fax)

3. *Approach national allied health care groups to seek NATA representation.*
4. *Approach payers on a national level to solicit support for reimbursement of certified athletic trainers.*
5. *Establish liaisons with appropriate groups to enhance the reimbursement efforts of certified athletic trainers.*

Table 3-5

REIMBURSEMENT ADVISORY GROUP COMMITTEE CONSULTANTS BY PRACTICE SETTINGS

Traditional Setting

Ivan Milton, ATC

Southwest Missouri State University

Athletic Training Services

Springfield, MO 65804

417-836-5461

417-836-6101 (fax)

iem348+@mail.smsu.edu

Clinical Setting

Terri Angelo, MA, ATC

Sports Medicine Specialist/Summa Health Systems

600 E Cuyahoga Falls Ave.

Akron, OH 44310

330-929-8541

330-929-7948 (fax)

Industrial Setting

Clark Simpson, MS, ATC

Community Hospitals—Indianapolis

8103 Clearvista, Suite 260

Indianapolis, IN 46256

317-588-7115

317-588-7117 (fax)

6. *Coordinate all reimbursement activities with the NATA Governmental Affairs Committee, the Clinical/Industrial/Corporate Committee, the Secondary School Committee, and the College/University Committee.*

It was further noted that reimbursement activity is predicted to increase at the college/university and secondary school levels, thus specific representation with these groups was important. Therefore, a liaison member to the RAG was added from the NATA Secondary School Committee and the NATA College/University Committee.

In 2000, several of the original RAG members completed their terms of committee service. New members were appointed and comprise the current committee (Table 3-6).

REIMBURSEMENT ADVISORY GROUP PUBLIC RELATIONS PLAN

A need was identified to educate clinic directors, practice managers, and hospital administrators responsible for hiring athletic trainers as to the benefit and value of these allied health professionals. To address that need, a specific reimbursement public relations plan was developed and implemented in October 2000. Components of that plan included an article focusing on athletic trainers as emerging health care providers published in a rehabilitation management magazine,[14] a specific brochure addressing why certified athletic trainers are valuable providers (see Appendix 6), letters of support from prominent physicians (see Appendix 7), and the NATA flyer "Unique Health Care Providers" (see Appendix 8). These materials were mailed directly to specific clinic directors, practice managers, and hospital administrators in target mailings.

Table 3-6

REIMBURSEMENT ADVISORY GROUP 2000

Chair

Marjorie J. Albohm, MS, ATC/L
Orthopaedics Indianapolis
1199 Hadley Rd.
Mooresville, IN 46158
317-831-2273
317-831-9347 (Fax)
mjalbohm@aol.com

Terri Angelo, MA, ATC/L
444 North Main St.
St. Thomas Hospital—Main 3
Akron, OH 44310
330-379-9544
330-379-9758 (Fax)

Timothy Auwarter, ATC/L '03
Tuomey Medical Park
1215 Alice Drive
Sumter, SC 29154
803-469-9811
gatorate@yahoo.com

Ann Berry, ATC/L '03
Tri-Rehab, Inc
15740 Michigan Ave.
Dearborn, MI 48126
313-584-7755
313-584-9628 (Fax)
abatc@aol.com

Jeff Konin, MEd, ATC/L, MPT
Delaware Tech Community College
P.O. Box 610
Owens Campus
Georgetown, DE 19947
302-856-5400
302-856-5773 (Fax)
jkonin@outland.dtec.edu

Marty Matney, MBA, ATC/L '03
13120 NE 70th Place, Suite 3
Kirkland, WA 98033
425-889-0776
425-889-0857
marty@whiteselprotherapy.edu

Tim McLane, MS, ATC/L '03
1600 Lakeland Hills Blvd.
Lakeland, FL 33805
863-680-7284
863-680-7542 (Fax)
tmclane@watsonclinic.com

Ivan Milton, ATC '03
Southwest Missouri State University
Athletic Training Services
Springfield, MO 65804
417-856-5461
417-835-6101 (Fax)
iem348+@mail.smsu.edu

Table 3-6 continued

Lou Rende, MS, ATC/L '03
The Center for Sports Medicine
1201 Nott St., Suite 302
Schenectady, NY 12308
518-243-4484
518-243-4342 (Fax)
lrende@thebiz.net

Clark Simpson, MS, ATC
8103 Clearvista Parkway, Suite 260
Indianapolis, IN 46256
317-588-7115
317-588-7117 (Fax)

NATA Committee Liaisons
Clinical/Industrial/Corporate
AT Committee
Sue Finkam, MS, ATC/L, CEA '04
Ergonomics Plus, Inc
8473 Pine Tree Blvd.
Indianapolis, IN 46256
317-849-4062
317-849-4062 (Fax)
sfinkam@ergo-plus.com

Governmental Affairs Committee
Keith J. Webster, MA, ATC/L '03
E J Nutter Training Facility
Room 136
Sports Center Drive

Lexington, KY 40506-0277
606-257-6521
606-257-8953 (Fax)
kjwebs@pop.uky.edu

Secondary School AT Committee
Jon L. Almquist, ATC/L
Fairfax County Public Schools
7731 Loosburg Pike
Falls Church, VA 22043
703-714-5466
703-714-5497 (Fax)
jlaatc@aol.com
Brian Robinson, ATC/L
Glenbrook South High School
4000 West Lake Ave.
Glenview, IL 60025
847-486-4600
847-486-4428 (Fax)
brobinson@glenbrook.k12.il.us

NATA Board of Directors Liaison
Thomas E. Koto, Jr, ATC/L
Idaho Sports Medicine Institute
1188 University Drive
Boise, ID 83706
208-395-8280
208-345-9514 (Fax)
tkoto@aol.com

Table 3-6 continued	
Nata Staff Liaisons	Richard Rogers, JD
Teresa Foster Welsh, MA	NATA
NATA	2952 Stemmons
2952 Stemmons	Dallas, TX 75247
Dallas, TX 75247	214-637-6282, ext. 103
214-637-6282, ext. 141	214-637-2206 (Fax)
214-637-2206 (Fax)	richr@nata.org
teresa@nata.org	

FOCUS GROUP

In November 2000, a Reimbursement Focus Group convened to address the questions most frequently asked by payers related to the benefit and value of athletic training as compared to other existing services provided. The group consisted of representatives from the NATA RAG, the NATA Governmental Affairs Committee, and the NATA Clinic/Industrial/Corporate Committee. The group was charged with developing an effective model for athletic training emphasizing benefit and value.

The unanimous consensus of the group was to develop and promote the model of the athletic trainer as a physician extender, emphasizing his or her unique skills and role as a clinical decision maker with the ability to provide a full continuum of patient care. A program was established, with supporting print materials, to introduce and promote this model with payers and other related constituents.

SUMMARY

Realizing the significance of the issue of third-party reimbursement for athletic trainers, the NATA created the RAG to advise and lead the association and its membership in the pursuit of this initiative. The group established goals and facilitated a nationwide outcomes study assessing care provided by certified athletic trainers. The group continues to provide leadership and direction in the pursuit of reimbursement for athletic trainers through specific goals, strategies, and initiatives.

REFERENCES

1. Iman A. Assessment and accountability: the third revolution in medical care. *N Engl J Med.* 1988;319:1220-1222.
2. Roper WL, Winkenwerder W, Hackbarth M, Krakauer H. Effectiveness in health care: an initiative to evaluate and improve medical practice. *N Engl J Med.* 1988;319:1197.
3. Berman GD, Kottke TE, Ballard DJ. Effectiveness research and assessment of clinical outcome: a review of federal government and medical community involvement. *Mayo Clin Proc.* 1990;65:657.
4. McCoy TH, Salvati EA, Ranawat CS, Wilson PD Jr. A 15-year follow-up study of 100 Charnley low-friction arthroplasties. *Orthop Clin North Am.* 1988;19:467.

IMPORTANT ITEMS TO INCLUDE WHEN APPROACHING THIRD-PARTY PAYERS

- Copy of the *NATA News*, 1990;September,2(4): "AMA Endorses Athletic Trainer as Allied Health Profession"
- Competencies in athletic training (from NATA)
- Copy of your state practice act
- Copy of your state Athletic Trainers' Association pamphlet and related state materials
- Copy of NATA membership invitation
- Copy of Research and Education Foundation information
- AMA–NATA Guidelines for Accreditation
- Any state proclamation or public relations (PR) handout
- Copies of *NATA News* articles relating to reimbursement

OTHER INFORMATION

- Find out the main contact person in the insurance company. Get an appointment with that person.
- When possible, have the meeting at your clinic. Provide a tour of your facility.
- Be prepared to answer questions as to why your profession should be included.
- Be prepared to talk prices. They may want athletic trainer services for less money than other professionals.
- Provide outcomes studies on athletic training if possible. Try to set this up with them if they provide you reimbursements.
- If you are with a hospital, check to see if it has a preferred provider organization (PPO). You could become a provider of services. The hospital would want to get the income for your services.

5. Peeler C. The future of physical therapy. *Rehab Management*. 1998;Dec/Jan:49.

6. Ellwood PM. Special report Shattuck lecture: outcomes management, a technology of patient experience. *N Engl J Med*. 1988;318:1549.

7. Brook RH, Lohr KN. Efficacy, effectiveness, variations and quality: boundary-crossing research. *Medical Care*. 1985;23:710-711.

8. Konin JG, ed. *Clinical Athletic Training*. Thorofare, NJ: SLACK Incorporated; 1997:246-251.

9. Donabadian A. Quality assessment and assurance; unity of purpose, diversity of means. *Inquiry.* 1988;25:173-192.

10. Gartland JJ. A shift in focus for orthopaedic clinical outcomes studies. *AAOS Bulletin.* 1990;30/31:4.

11. Albohm MJ, Wilkerson GB. An outcomes assessment of care provided by certified athletic trainers. *J Rehabil Outcomes Meas.* 1999;3(3):51-56.

12. Focus on Therapeutic Outcomes, Inc. *Comparitive Analysis.* Knoxville, Tenn: Focus on Therapeutic Outcomes Inc.; 1999.

13. The State of Georgia House Bill 93, Georgia 145th General Assembly, 1999-00 Regular Session, April 19, 1999.

14. Albohm MJ. On your mark—-changes in reimbursement and legislation promise bright future for ATCs. *Advance News Magazine.* 2000;9(10):25-26.

Chapter Four

The Basics of Claims Filing

OBJECTIVES

Following the completion of this chapter, the reader will be able to:
- Define and recognize appropriate use of current procedural terminology (CPT) codes.
- Become familiar with provider numbers designated for reimbursement.
- Identify the appropriate forms needed for reimbursement.
- Follow the necessary steps for preparation of filing a claim.
- List the most common reasons for claims denial.
- Create a process for appealing denied claims.
- Develop effective communication techniques for dealing with third-party payers.
- List four types of outcomes related to reimbursement efforts.
- Discuss future trends in claims filing.

INTRODUCTION

The process of delivering money in exchange for a service has been a long-established form of business. Reimbursement has been historically defined as a numerical value of currency that one is entitled to in exchange for the delivery of services.[1] In health care, any form of reimbursement from a third-party payer comes as no simple task. Arguably the most important component to ensuring financial compensation for the delivery of athletic training services is what has come to be known as "claims filing." Claims filing is a process whereby health care providers submit appropriate documentation to a third-party payer, who in return reviews the material prior to making a decision regarding the extent of reimbursable services. Since there is an increased competition among all providers for the limited dollars that are available for reimbursable services, successful filing of a claim becomes critical to the financial survival of any athletic trainer who depends on third-party payers as a source of income.

CURRENT PROCEDURAL TERMINOLOGY

In an attempt to standardize the many types of services that may be rendered by health care professionals, the American Medical Association (AMA) has established what is known as current procedural terminology, or CPT codes.[2-4] These procedures are labeled using five-digit codes that are standardized nationally (Table 4-1). The codes are developed by the AMA in consultation with an allied health advisory board, which at the present time includes no athletic trainers. Allied health professionals representing the fields of medicine, physical therapy, occupational therapy, speech/language pathology, physician's assisting, nursing, social work, and podiatry comprise the advisory board.[2,3]

Table 4-1

EXAMPLE OF CPT CODING

97010—Application of a modality to one or more areas: hot or cold packs

97012—Traction, mechanical

97014—Electrical stimulation (unattended)

97016—Vasopneumatic devices

97018—Paraffin bath

97020—Microwave

97022—Whirlpool

97024—Diathermy

97026—Infrared

97028—Ultraviolet

Despite the absence of an athletic trainer on the AMA's advisory board, athletic trainers may use CPT codes for the purpose of reimbursement.[5] In the Physical Medicine section of the CPT coding book, the AMA clearly identifies a "provider" of these services as a general term used to define the individual providing the service described in the code.[5] The provider can be anyone who is licensed or certified to perform the service. Thus, with proper credentials and favorable licenser, athletic trainers are included in utilization of these codes. CPT codes commonly utilized by certified athletic trainers are listed in Table 4-2.

When using CPT codes to denote a service rendered, it is important to recognize that the determination of payment policy regarding various third-party payers is solely dependent upon each party's decision-making process. In other words, athletic trainers may complete appropriate paperwork outlining the services rendered via CPT coding terms, yet no reimbursement is guaranteed until the third-party payer accepts the service rendered as justifiable in its own terms.[1,5]

INTERNATIONAL CLASSIFICATION OF DISEASES

Reimbursement through a third-party payer not only involves a series of codes used to identify a service rendered, it also involves a series of codes used to identify a patient's diagnosis. These codes are referred to as the International Classification of Diseases, or ICD.[6] ICD codes are accepted by most private insurance agencies as a way of keeping consistent and standardized methods of classifying an injury.[2,4] Regardless of the provider rendering care, the ICD used for a patient would be the same throughout one's treatment process. For example, a patient who has been treated for lateral epicondylitis by a physician may be sent to an athletic trainer for rehabilitation of the overuse injury. When submitting a claim for reimbursement, both the physician and the athletic trainer would use the same ICD code since they are treating the identical injury. What they would code differently would be the type of treatment that each rendered. Thus, they would most likely use different CPT codes. Third-party payers, such as Medicare, will check to see that the treatments rendered are appropriate for the diagnosis that is coded.[7]

Table 4-2

DESCRIPTION OF PHYSICAL MEDICINE
CHARGES USED BY ATHLETIC TRAINERS

The following is a guide to CPT codes that may be used by athletic trainers when billing for athletic training services. It is important to have the proper ICD-9 diagnosis code prior to using the CPT codes. The current information is in reference to 1999 CPT codes.

Evaluation Charges

97799—Sports Medicine/or Athletic Trainer Evaluation (Per Visit)
Used for evaluation of athletic injuries to determine the appropriate plan of care by a regulated athletic trainer. (97799—Unlisted physical medicine/rehabilitation service or procedure.)

97750—Physical Performance Test (Each 15 Minutes)
Used when performing specific musculoskeletal examination, such as specific muscle strength, closed chain testing, vestibular/balance testing, isokinetic testing, or other physical performance testing. Must have a written report/documentation to support this (eg, physician progress report for patient visit). Also used for functional capacity evaluations (each 15 minutes).

97001—Physical Therapy Evaluation
Used if the athletic training is being provided as a means of physical rehabilitation to assist the patient in recovering from an injury or illness. The athletic trainer must be a state-licensed health care professional in order to use this code (per the CPT Information Services).

Treatment Charges

97116—Gait Training (Each 15 Minutes)
Used when performing gait training activities, including stair climbing, with patients.

97110—Therapeutic Exercise (Each 15 Minutes)
Used when performing therapeutic exercises to develop strength and endurance, ROM, and flexibility to one or more areas (each 15 minutes). One-on-one interaction with patient (eg, use this charge when performing initial ACL quad vastus medialis obliquis (vmo) and ROM exercises or performing lumbar stabilization with the goal of strengthening muscles).

97112—Neuromuscular Re-education (Each 15 Minutes)
Used when performing neuromuscular re-education of movement, balance coordination, kinesthetic sense, posture, and proprioception.

97530—Therapeutic Activities (Each 15 Minutes)
Direct patient contact using dynamic activities to improve functional mobility, like physical and sports activities.

97113—Aquatic Therapeutic Exercise (Each 15 Minutes)
This charge is used for aquatic therapy when using the pool.

Table 4-2 continued

97124—Massage (Each 15 Minutes)
Used when performing massage including, but not limited to, effleurage, petrissage, and/or tapotement (stroking, compression, percussion).

97530—Body Mechanics Training (Each 15 Minutes)
Used when performing therapeutic activities to train a person on proper body mechanics in order to improve functional performance.

97140—Manual Therapy (Each 15 Minutes)
Used when joint mobilization, manual lymphatic drainage, manual traction, myofascial release, craniosacral, soft tissue mobilization, or desensitization techniques are utilized.

97504—Orthotics Fitting and Training (Each 15 Minutes)
Used for orthotic training (dynamic bracing, splinting) for upper and lower extremities. (This charge should not be used in addition to a gait training charge.)

97150—Therapeutic Procedures—Group (Each Visit)
Used when working with two or more individuals at one time on therapeutic activities/exercises. May be used with other charges. Group lumbar stabilization, group aquatic therapy, or group exercise programs should use this charge.

97150—Supervised Exercise (Each Visit)
Used when the patient requires minimal supervision with his or her exercise program or used in services needed but not directly provided by licensed personnel. (Less than 1 hour and greater than 1 hour are two separate possible charges.)

11040—Debridement (Each Visit)
Used when performing debridement procedures in conjunction with wound care (check scope of practice for state).

97139—Wound Care (Each 15 Minutes)
Used when performing dressing changes and wound care activities other than debridement. Or more specifically (when debridement is included):

16020—Burn Debridement and/or Dressing, 9% or Less

16025—Burn Debridement and/or Dressing, 10% to 18%

16030—Burn Debridement and/or Dressing, 19% or More

97139—Taping (Each Visit)

Charge for taping of patient during treatment session; taping shoulder, knee, ankle, etc. Or more specifically:

29240—Shoulder Strapping/Taping

29260—Elbow/Wrist Strapping/Taping

29280—Hand/Finger Strapping/Taping

29520—Hip Strapping/Taping

29530—Knee Strapping/Taping

Table 4-2 continued

29540—Ankle Strapping/Taping

29550—Toes Strapping/Taping

29580—Unna Boot

95831—Manual Muscle Testing—Extremity/Trunk

95832— Manual Muscle Testing Hand with/without Comparison with Normal Side

95833— Manual Muscle Testing Total Evaluation of Body, Excluding Hands

95837— Manual Muscle Testing Evaluation of Body, Including Hands

95851—ROM—of Measurements and Report (Separate Procedure), Each Extremity (Excluding Hand), or Each Trunk Section (Spine)

95852—ROM Measurements of Hand, with/without Comparison with Normal Side

97545—Work Hardening/Conditioning; Initial 2 Hours

97546—Work Hardening/Conditioning; Each Additional Hour (List Separately in Addition to Code for Primary Procedure)

Modalities

97035—Ultrasound (Each 15 Minutes)
Deep heat modality used to decrease pain and muscle spasm.

97035—Phonophoresis (Each 15 Minutes)
This charge is used when performing ultrasound treatment using medication (usually a steroid) to help decrease pain and inflammation.

97032—Electrical Stimulation (Each 15 Minutes)
Used for treatment of trigger points and muscle spasms to treat specific areas of pain using a combination of both ultrasound and electrical stimulation at the same time.

97033—Iontophoresis (Each 15 Minutes)
Electrical stimulation that is used to drive a medication into the tissue. Used to decrease pain and inflammation. Includes the cost for medication, electrodes, and direct therapy time.

97032—Constant Electrical Stimulation (Each 15 Minutes)
Used for treatment of trigger points for pain reduction, motor points for muscle re-education, or any other electrical stimulation that requires direct (one-on-one) patient contract by the provider.

97034—Contrast Baths (Each 15 Minutes)
Modality used to help with edema/pain reduction.

97014—Electrical Stimulation (Application to One or More Areas)
Used for pain modification, muscle spasm reduction, and edema reduction. It is used when there does not have to be constant attendance by the provider through the whole treatment procedure. Charged by the visit.

Table 4-2 continued

97022—Whirlpool (Application to One or More Areas)
Used for treatment of wounds/debridement, pain reduction, muscle relaxation, edema reduction, and improving ROM. Charge by the visit.

97010—Hot Packs (Application to One or More Areas)
Application of moist heat pack used for pain modulation muscle relaxation. Can only bill for this if used in conjunction with another therapy treatment or modality. Charged by the visit.

97010—Cold Packs/Ice Massage (Application to One or More Areas)
Application of cold pack or performance of ice massage to one or more areas used for pain reduction, edema reduction, or muscle spasm reduction. Can only bill for this if used in conjunction with another therapy treatment or modality. Charged by the visit.

97012—Traction, Mechanical (Not Time Based)
Cervical or lumbar traction used to help decrease pain and improve mobility. Charged by the visit.

97016—Compression Pump (Application to One or More Areas)
Vasopneumatic modality used for edema reduction.

Other Procedures

Continuous Passive Motion Set-Up (Per Visit)
Set-up of CPM machine on patient (shoulder, knee, or wrist). Includes time to adjust to right setting, patient education, and evaluation of patient's tolerance. Documentation of this service will be found in evaluation or daily progress note.

Continuous Passive Motion Daily (Per Visit)
Daily assessment of CPM machine to ensure proper fit, speed, and ROM settings. Also to evaluate patient's tolerance to treatment. Documentation of this activity will be found in daily progress note.

DOCUMENTATION

Documentation is the hallmark of successful reimbursement. There are many possible reasons as to whether or not a claim will be reimbursed. However, without thorough and timely documentation, one's chances for third-party payer cooperation are diminished. Proper documentation involves paying attention to details, providing accurate and comprehensive facts, and abiding by the policies and procedures of the third-party payers.

While many insurance companies may have their own forms, there are some common pieces of paperwork that are standard to the industry. There are also forms that may be created by an individual facility or practice that will help achieve successful reimbursement.

Patient Registration Form

The patient registration form is typically the first document that a patient will complete prior to any rendering of services. Information on this form includes the patient's name, address, phone number, emergency phone number, and insurance information. It may also include such pieces of data as any allergies that a patient may have, questions regarding their injury, questions about past medical history, and any other pertinent information that a facility may require.[4]

Patient Encounter Form

An encounter form is used by the provider to document each individual patient visit. This is not a nationally standardized form, but rather a customized form by each facility or practice. A patient encounter form is most commonly used for the purposes of daily patient data entry and therefore should contain such information as commonly used CPT codes and diagnosis codes in a checklist design. Patient encounter forms may need to be made in replicate since patients may submit these directly to their own insurance companies. As a result, it is imperative that all proper information is available in the creation of a patient encounter form (Figure 4-1).

Daily Journal

A daily journal allows for a facility to keep a chronological summary of all of the charges posted to patient accounts on a daily basis. Design of such a form should consider not only the posted charges, but also dates and payments received. A daily journal becomes important in tracking and monitoring accounts receivable. This form is most useful from a business perspective of services and helps to determine revenue based upon a calendar observation.

Individual Patient Account

An individual patient account form is simply a summary of an individual patient's accounts receivable. A thorough form that includes diagnosis, date of service, services rendered, charges posted, and charges received will help one to keep updated and accurate records of the patient's account status.

Treatment Note

There are many forms of treatment notes ranging from a subjective, objective, assessment, plan (SOAP) note format to a narrative style of documentation. Regardless of choice, the treatment note is a complete description of the patient's encounter per each treatment session. It should clearly include the date, the patient's initial comments and/or observations prior to treatment, the type and length of treatment rendered, the patient's and the clinician's response following the treatment, and the stated plan of action as it relates to the patient's outlined goals. All observations, findings, and goals should be related to practical and functional expectations.[8]

Insurance Claim Forms

Insurance claim forms are the actual forms that need to be submitted to third-party payers for reimbursement purposes. Standard forms that exist include the HCFA-1500 (Figure 4-2) derived for the purpose of Medicare reimbursement, and the UB-92 (Figure 4-3) used by Blue Cross/Blue Shield for reimbursement of rehabilitative services and durable medical equipment. It is quite possible that a facility can create its own form for submitting a claim that is inclusive of all pertinent information; however, most insurance companies will not accept the claim unless it is completed on the individual insurance company's form.

STEPS FOR FILING A CLAIM

The process whereby one "files a claim" does not have any specific order. Rather, the completeness of information included within a claim is of greater importance. A large portion of the data that is

DATE	PATIENT NO.	CHARGES	CREDITS	CUR. BALANCE	PREV BALANCE	NAME

PAID BY   ☐ CASH   ☐ VISA/MC   ☐ CHECK

OFFICE NEW PATIENT

99201	LEVEL 1
99202	LEVEL 2
99203	LEVEL 3
99204	LEVEL 4
99205	LEVEL 5

OFFICE ESTABLISHED PT

99211	LEVEL 1
99212	LEVEL 2
99213	LEVEL 3
99214	LEVEL 4
99215	LEVEL 5
200	POST OP/NC

OFFICE OUTPATIENT CONSULTATION

99241	LEVEL 1
99242	LEVEL 2
99243	LEVEL 3
99244	LEVEL 4
99245	LEVEL 5

CONFIRMATORY CONSULTATION

99271	LEVEL 1
99272	LEVEL 2
99273	LEVEL 3
99274	LEVEL 4
99275	LEVEL 5

X-RAY SPINE & PELVIS

72010	ENTIRE, AP & LAT
72020	SPINE, 1V
72040	CERVICAL, AP & LAT
72050	CERVICAL, 4V
72052	CERVICAL, COMPLETE, 6V
72070	THORACIC, AP & LAT
72080	THORACOLUMBAR SPINE,
72100	LUMBOSACRAL, AP & LAT
72110	LUMBOSACRAL, 4V
72170	PELVIS, AP ONLY
73520	PELVIS W/LAT HIP
72220	SACRUM & COCCYX 2V
72200	SACROILIAC JOINTS
72190	PELVIS COMP 3V

LOWER EXTREMITY

73500	HIP, UNILAT, 1V
73510	HIP, COMP. 2V
73550	FEMUR, AP & LAT
73560	KNEE, 1V
73560	KNEE, AP & LAT
73562	KNEE, 3V
73564	KNEE, 4V
73590	TIBIA & FIBULA, AP & LAT
73600	ANKLE, AP & LAT
73610	ANKLE, COMP 3V
73650	CALCANEUS, MIN 2V
73660	TOES MIN 2V
73062	STANDING LEG
73620	FOOT AP & LAT
73630	FOOT COMP 3V

UPPER EXTREMITY

73000	CLAVICLE, COMPLETE
71130	STERNOCLAV-JNTS, COMP
73010	SCAPULA, COMPLETE
73020	SHOULDER, 1V
73030	SHOULDER, 2V
193	SHOULDER, 3V ROUTINE
73050	AC JOINT, 2V
221	AC JOINT, BILAT 4V
73060	HUMEROUS, 2V
73070	ELBOW, AP & LAT
73080	ELBOW, COMP. 3V ROUTINE
73090	FOREARM, AP & LAT
73100	WRIST, AP & LAT
73110	WRIST, 3V
218	WRIST, 5V ROUTINE
219	WRIST, 6V
73120	HAND, 2V
73130	HAND, MIN 3V
73140	FINGER, MIN 2V

BILATERAL

156	X/R ANKLE 2 VW(AP/LAT)
157	X/R ANKLE 3VW
160	X/R CALC. 2 VW
162	X/R ELBOW 2 VW
163	X/R ELBOW 3 VW
169	X/R FEMUR 2 VW
133	X/R FOOT 1 VW LAT
159	X/R FOOT 3 VW
276	X/R FOOT AP'LAT 2 VW
164	X/R FOREARM 2 VW
168	X/R HAND 3 VW
167	X/R HAND 2 VW
161	X/R HUMERUS 2 VW
155	X/R TIB & FIB 2 VW
165	X/R WRIST 2 VW(AP/LAT)
166	X/R WRIST 3 VW
170	X/R KNEE 3 VW OR LESS
170	X/R KNEE 4 VW OR MORE
278	COMP PRESS ACUTE
277	X/R SHLDR 3 VW OR LESS
221	X/R AC JNT 4 VW OR MORE
224	X/R STANDING LEG BIL
286	X/R KNEE 4V ORBIT

MISCELLANEOUS

71010	CHEST, 1V
71020	CHEST, 2V
71100	RIBS, 2V
71110	RIBS, BILAT
71120	STERNUM, 2V
76499	X-RAY COPY
76140	REVIEW OUTSIDE X-RAY
93000	EKG

INJECTION ASPIRATION

20600	SMALL JOINT
20605	INTERMEDIATE JOINT
20610	LARGE JOINT

NEW PATIENT-PT

97799	EVAL-NEW PAT 30 MIN
00201	PT OFFICE VISIT-NC

PROCEDURES

64550	APPL OF TENS UNIT
97116	GAIT TRAINING
97124	MASSAGE
97250	MYOFAS REL/SOFT TIS MOB
97112	NEUROMUSCULAR RE-ED
97530	THERAP ACTIV.-15 MIN
97110	THERAP EXERC.-15 MIN
97122	TRACTION-MANUAL

MODALITIES

97032	ELECTRICAL STIM.-15 MIN
97010	HOT PACK/COLD PACK
97033	IONTOPHORESIS - 15 MIN
97012	TRACTION - MECHANICAL
97035	ULTRASOUND-15 MIN
97016	VASOPNEUMATIC DEVICE
97022	WHIRLPOOL

TESTS & MEASUREMENTS

97750	PHYS. PERF TEST-15 MIN
95851	KT 1000
20950(101)	C. P. TEST MULT/BILAT
20950	C. P. TEST-SINGLE
20950(100)	C. P. TEST-MULTI OR BILAT.

CASTS

29065	LONG ARM
29075	SHORT ARM
29085	HAND TO LOWER ARM
29345	LONG LEG
29365	CYLINDER CAST
29405	SHORT LEG
29425	SHORT LEG-WALKING
29700	CAST REMOVAL/BIVALVING
29085	THUMB CAST

SPLINTS

29130	A4570 FINGER SPLINT
29125(249)	A4570 HAND BASED SPLT
29105	A4570 LONG ARM SPLINT
29125	A4570 SHORT ARM SPLINT
29125(259)	A4570 SHORT ARM SPL(PC)
29515	A4570 SHORT LEG SPLINT
29126(257)	A4570 DYN. PRO SPLNT SUP
29126	A4570 LARGE DYN. SPLINT
29131(186)	A4570 SAFETY PIN SPLINT
29131	A4570 SMALL DYN. SPLINT
29105(275)	A4570 MUNSTER SPLINT

STRAPPING

29540	A4454 STRAP ANKLE
29260	A4454 STRP ELB/WRIST
29280	A4454 HAND/FINGER
29520	A4454 STRAP HIP
29530	A4454 STRAP KNEE
29240	A4454 STRAP SHOULDER
29550	A4454 STRAP FOOT/TOES

MEDICAL SUPPLIES

L4350	AIRCAST-STD
L4370	AIRCAST-LONG
L4360	AC-WALK.BOOT
A4570(151)	AC TEN-ELB STRAP
106	CAST SHOE
L3670	CLAVICLE STRAP
L3914	CTR."RC" WRIST BR
L3914(152)	CTR."RU" WRIST BR
E0112	CRUTCHES
E0237	CRYOCUFF
L3690(132)	DANEK AC IMMOB.
L1815	DJ HINGED KNEE BR
A4565	FASHION SLING
L3040	FOOT ARCH SPPT
E1399(254)	GEL ANTI-VIB GLOVE
E1399(187)	HAND EXER. AID
L1830	KNEE IMMOBILIZER
E1399(284)	LIONS PAW
L3020	LANGER ORTHO.
E1399(111)	LUMBAR/CERV ROLL
L0515	LUMBO/SAC SUPPT.
L4210	ORTHO. REFURBISH
E1399(179)	PRO CALF SLEEVE
L1800(226)	PRO DR. M KNEE BR
L1800	PRO DR.MU BRACE
A4570	PRO ELBOW SLEEVE
L3710	PRO ELB HNGED BR
L8190	PRO EXER. TRUNK
L1810	PRO HNG KNEE BR
L1800(110)	PRO KNEE SLEEVE
L1825	PRO OSGOOD STRP
E1399(115)	PRO THIGH SLVE.
L3650(233)	SHOULDER PULLEY
L3650(150)	SHOULDER IMMOB.
L3650(245)	SHLD'R REHAB. KIT
L3960	SHLD'R SUBL INHIB.
L3660	SHLD'R SAWA BR.
L1960	SWEDO ANKLE BR.

NEXT APPT.	DAY	DATE	TIME	CODE
Dr.				
PT				
DIAG.			DOI	

Figure 4-1. Patient encounter form. (reprinted with permission from Konin JG, ed. *Clinical Athletic Training.* Thorofare, NJ: SLACK Incorporated; 1997:97).

PLEASE DO NOT STAPLE IN THIS AREA

CARRIER

PICA

HEALTH INSURANCE CLAIM FORM

PICA

1. MEDICARE (Medicare #) MEDICAID (Medicaid #) CHAMPUS (Sponsor's SSN) CHAMPVA (VA File #) GROUP HEALTH PLAN (SSN or ID) FECA BLK LUNG (SSN) OTHER (ID)

1a. INSURED'S I.D. NUMBER (FOR PROGRAM IN ITEM 1)

2. PATIENT'S NAME (Last Name, First Name, Middle Initial)

3. PATIENT'S BIRTH DATE MM DD YY SEX M F

4. INSURED'S NAME (Last Name, First Name, Middle Initial)

5. PATIENT'S ADDRESS (No., Street)

6. PATIENT RELATIONSHIP TO INSURED Self Spouse Child Other

7. INSURED'S ADDRESS (No., Street)

CITY STATE

8. PATIENT STATUS Single Married Other

CITY STATE

ZIP CODE TELEPHONE (Include Area Code) ( )

Employed Full-Time Student Part-Time Student

ZIP CODE TELEPHONE (INCLUDE AREA CODE) ( )

9. OTHER INSURED'S NAME (Last Name, First Name, Middle Initial)

10. IS PATIENT'S CONDITION RELATED TO:

11. INSURED'S POLICY GROUP OR FECA NUMBER

a. OTHER INSURED'S POLICY OR GROUP NUMBER

a. EMPLOYMENT? (CURRENT OR PREVIOUS) YES NO

a. INSURED'S DATE OF BIRTH MM DD YY SEX M F

b. OTHER INSURED'S DATE OF BIRTH MM DD YY SEX M F

b. AUTO ACCIDENT? PLACE (State) YES NO

b. EMPLOYER'S NAME OR SCHOOL NAME

c. EMPLOYER'S NAME OR SCHOOL NAME

c. OTHER ACCIDENT? YES NO

c. INSURANCE PLAN NAME OR PROGRAM NAME

d. INSURANCE PLAN NAME OR PROGRAM NAME

10d. RESERVED FOR LOCAL USE

d. IS THERE ANOTHER HEALTH BENEFIT PLAN? YES NO *If yes*, return to and complete item 9 a-d.

READ BACK OF FORM BEFORE COMPLETING & SIGNING THIS FORM.

12. PATIENT'S OR AUTHORIZED PERSON'S SIGNATURE I authorize the release of any medical or other information necessary to process this claim. I also request payment of government benefits either to myself or to the party who accepts assignment below.

SIGNED ________ DATE ________

13. INSURED'S OR AUTHORIZED PERSON'S SIGNATURE I authorize payment of medical benefits to the undersigned physician or supplier for services described below.

SIGNED ________

PATIENT AND INSURED INFORMATION

14. DATE OF CURRENT: MM DD YY ILLNESS (First symptom) OR INJURY (Accident) OR PREGNANCY (LMP)

15. IF PATIENT HAS HAD SAME OR SIMILAR ILLNESS. GIVE FIRST DATE MM DD YY

16. DATES PATIENT UNABLE TO WORK IN CURRENT OCCUPATION FROM MM DD YY TO MM DD YY

17. NAME OF REFERRING PHYSICIAN OR OTHER SOURCE

17a. I.D. NUMBER OF REFERRING PHYSICIAN

18. HOSPITALIZATION DATES RELATED TO CURRENT SERVICES FROM MM DD YY TO MM DD YY

19. RESERVED FOR LOCAL USE

20. OUTSIDE LAB? YES NO $ CHARGES

21. DIAGNOSIS OR NATURE OF ILLNESS OR INJURY. (RELATE ITEMS 1,2,3 OR 4 TO ITEM 24E BY LINE)

1. ___ . ___ 3. ___ . ___

2. ___ . ___ 4. ___ . ___

22. MEDICAID RESUBMISSION CODE ORIGINAL REF. NO.

23. PRIOR AUTHORIZATION NUMBER

24. A DATE(S) OF SERVICE From MM DD YY To MM DD YY	B Place of Service	C Type of Service	D PROCEDURES, SERVICES, OR SUPPLIES (Explain Unusual Circumstances) CPT/HCPCS MODIFIER	E DIAGNOSIS CODE	F $ CHARGES	G DAYS OR UNITS	H EPSDT Family Plan	I EMG	J COB	K RESERVED FOR LOCAL USE
1										
2										
3										
4										
5										
6										

25. FEDERAL TAX I.D. NUMBER SSN EIN

26. PATIENT'S ACCOUNT NO.

27. ACCEPT ASSIGNMENT? (For govt. claims see back) YES NO

28. TOTAL CHARGE $

29. AMOUNT PAID $

30. BALANCE DUE $

31. SIGNATURE OF PHYSICIAN OR SUPPLIER INCLUDING DEGREES OR CREDENTIALS (I certify that the statements on the reverse apply to this bill and are made a part thereof.)

SIGNED DATE

32. NAME AND ADDRESS OF FACILITY WHERE SERVICES WERE RENDERED (If other than home or office)

33. PHYSICIAN'S, SUPPLIER'S BILLING NAME, ADDRESS, ZIP CODE & PHONE #

PIN# GRP#

PHYSICIAN OR SUPPLIER INFORMATION

(APPROVED BY AMA COUNCIL ON MEDICAL SERVICE 8/88)

PLEASE PRINT OR TYPE

APPROVED OMB-0938-0008 FORM HCFA-1500 (12-90), FORM RRB-1500, APPROVED OMB-1215-0055 FORM OWCP-1500, APPROVED OMB-0720-0001 (CHAMPUS)

Figure 4-2. HCFA-1500 form. (reprinted with permission from Konin JG, ed. *Clinical Athletic Training*. Thorofare, NJ: SLACK Incorporated; 1997:99.).

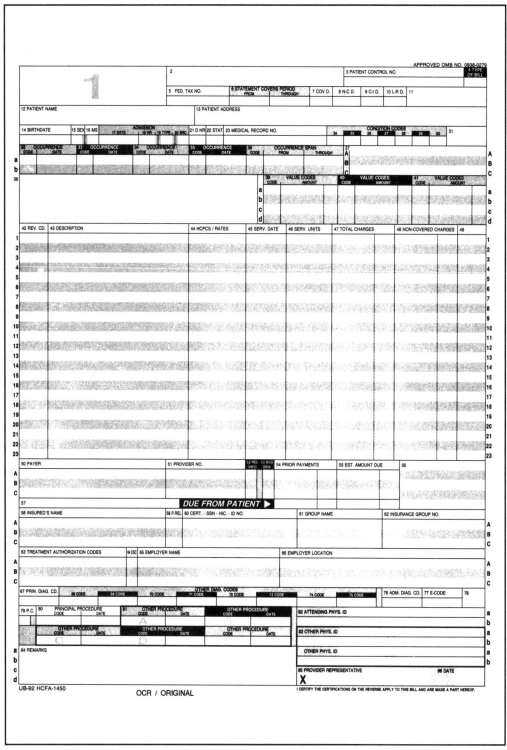

Figure 4-3. UB-92 form. (reprinted with permission from Konin JG, ed. *Clinical Athletic Training*. Thorofare, NJ: SLACK Incorporated; 1997:100.).

needed to complete an accurate claim is gathered from the moment the patient walks into the facility. Forms that have been discussed previously, such as the patient encounter form, may provide relevant information necessary to complete a claim.

Preparation

The most important step in filing a claim is preparation. It becomes critically important to the effort of reimbursement that one prepares to gather all relevant information before, during, and after treatment has been rendered, yet before a claim is submitted.[9] Having a thorough knowledge of what the major insurance carriers often ask for serves to be beneficial for the filer.[10] These questions can therefore be transferred to patient encounter and patient registration forms, making data collection much easier and reducing the time spent searching for information.

Review

Further review of all documents prior to officially filing them will allow for individual facilities to screen for errors that may trigger third-party denial. This process, referred to as "in-house utilization review," involves health care providers analyzing each other's paperwork in an attempt to:
- Improve documentation
- Standardize terminology
- Assess appropriateness of the plan of care
- Determine further necessity of treatment, among other issues[7]

Submission

Sending a claim to the appropriate address may sound simplistic, but it is not uncommon for claims to be lost or sent to different departments of an insurance company. Therefore, after spending valuable time ensuring that a claim is complete and accurate, be sure to ascertain a correct address and preferably a receiver's name for safe delivery. Though costly, it may not be wise to send claims via certified mail, which requires a signature.

DENIAL OF A CLAIM

It is the responsibility of each and every health care provider filing an insurance claim to have all of the necessary documentation submitted to the third-party payer in a timely fashion without any missing information. It seems logical that if an athletic trainer was to accurately complete a claim and submit it to the appropriate party, then reimbursement would occur. However, this is most often not the case. Regardless of a provider's knowledge and attention to detail with regard to a claim, often times relevant information may be overlooked and missing.[7] In fact, sometimes information that is considered to be irrelevant by the provider, but required by the insurance company, may be omitted and lead to a claim denial.[11]

Reimbursement for athletic training services involves the completion of proper, adequate, thorough, and timely documentation. It is the athletic trainer's responsibility to communicate in writing a clear and appropriate picture of the services provided so that third-party payers can understand and assess the potential for reimbursement. Common mistakes made when filing a claim can be divided into four categories (Table 4-3):
1. Appropriateness
2. Completeness
3. Compliance
4. Timeliness[12]

Table 4-3

COMMON MISTAKES LEADING TO CLAIM DENIAL

Appropriateness
Inappropriate service rendered
Unnecessary service rendered
Treatment not matching physician's orders
No pre-certification
Lack of progress of patient

Completeness
Improper forms
Lack of clear description of progress
Lack of client information
Poor quality note
Illegible documentation
Improper coding
Incomplete forms and documentation
No physician referral

Compliance
No home program established or followed
Unrealistic goals
Nonfunctional goals
Unsafe delivery of services
Not following third-party payer guidelines
Patient noncompliance
Lack of progress
Lack of re-evaluations
Patient absence of treatment sessions

Timeliness
Treatment administered too soon
Tardy documentation
Late filing of claim
Outdated prescriptions
Excessively long duration of care

Appropriateness

The first and foremost consideration of a third-party payer is whether or not the service provided is appropriate and necessary. This includes the delivery of hands-on treatment, the use of therapeutic modalities, and the amount, frequency, and duration of the services.[7,10] All treatment should match the physician's orders as well as the functional and realistic goals set forth at the beginning of the delivery of services. Precertification—the process of receiving verbal and/or written approval by a third-party payer prior to the initiation of treatment, acknowledging reimbursement of services—is also important. This not only guarantees the athletic trainer that the payer has approved the delivery of services, but also screens for additional denial criteria, such as duplication of services, whereby a person may have already been treated in the same manner for the same injury by a different facility or clinician. Maintenance of a condition or lack of progress will not be reimbursed.

Completeness

All claims should be submitted on the proper forms that are requested by each and every individual third-party payer. Furthermore, the completion of these forms is essential, as any missing piece of information may be critical to the third-party payer's decision-making process as to whether or not it should reimburse for a designated service. The following are common reasons for being denied reimbursement on the basis of an incomplete claim:
- No physician referral
- Improper forms used
- Improper coding
- Illegible documentation
- Poor quality note

- Lack of client information
- Lack of clear description of progress

Compliance

Reimbursement depends partly on the compliance of both the provider and the recipient of services. Compliance on behalf of the provider, in this case the athletic trainer, involves issues such as establishing, following, and regularly monitoring realistic and functional goals of the client. It also includes delivering professional and safe care, documenting such services, and appropriately filing the claim according to the guidelines set forth by the third-party payer. The recipient of the services must demonstrate a compliant effort on his or her behalf to improve and progress in a reasonable and timely manner that corresponds to the nature and severity of the injury or illness at hand. Lack of progress, lack of re-evaluations, absence of treatment sessions, and minimal compliance to rehabilitation outside of the supervised setting may also lead to concerns on behalf of the payer. Thus, preparation and education may prevent situations that may ultimately result in a denial of reimbursement.

Timeliness

Treatment initiated prior to precertification, documentation and claims filed beyond agreed upon timeliness, outdated prescriptions, excessively long durations of care, and many other temporal-related outcomes may also result in a denial of reimbursement. These issues are all avoidable mistakes and simply involve attention to detail. Mistakes made in this category of claims filing are particularly frustrating, as they do not necessarily result directly from the delivery of care, but rather from the administrative component of the delivery of services.

APPEALING DENIED CLAIMS

Unfortunately, it is a common occurrence that clams are denied. However, one should not rest with the judgment of a claims denial, as the rationale behind the denial may be explained and corrected in further correspondence. Before discussing the appeal process, those denials that are not appealable need to be mentioned. On most occasions, dollar values that are reimbursed are not subject to negotiation.[13] The value determined is typically based on a preset fee by the insurance carrier. Any services provided that are not covered in a patient's or insurance provider's plan are also closed to negotiation. Whenever care plans are not followed, deadlines are not met, or procedures are performed that were not ordered or are not justifiable, claims will be denied on the basis of noncompliance.

Ashby describes a process referred to as denial process management (DPM), which is designed to offset denials.[14] The plan consists of tracking and analyzing the number of denied claims and the reasons that they were denied. The goal of DPM is to establish patterns that will help providers predict which claims will be paid, which will trigger denials, and which denials are likely to be overturned on appeal.

When you have determined that a denied claim is deserving of an appeal, you must be very clear in your reasoning for the appeal as well as the expectations you are seeking from the third-party payer. In doing so, you need to gather all relevant documentation, review the paperwork related to both the services provided as well as the rules and regulations of the third-party payer, and design a cover letter that succinctly explains your concern. All of this needs to be done in a timely matter. A good cover letter includes the following pieces of information:[10,13]

- Facility name, address, and phone number
- Date of appeal
- Reminder of original date of claims submission

Table 4-4

TIPS FOR ENHANCING COMMUNICATION WITH NONCLINICIAN REVIEWERS

- Use universally understood medical terminology.
- If using grades or rating in your reports, provide a scale of average/normative values.
- Speak in practical and functional terms.
- Use outlines and charts instead of long-winded narratives.
- Reduce repetition of information to a minimum.

- Recipient's name and address
- Provider's name, address, and provider number or tax identification number
- Patient's name, address, phone number, and insurer identification number
- Date of service and total charges
- Claim number
- Reiterate the reason for denial
- Explanation of why charges should be paid

COMMUNICATION WITH THIRD-PARTY PAYERS

A significant part of successful reimbursement revolves around communication between the provider and the insurer.[15,16] Most of the individuals with which the provider will deal from the third-party payer organizations will not have any formalized training, inservice, or education to assist them with understanding what athletic training is, what constitutes the need for athletic training services, how effective athletic trainers are, what diagnoses athletic trainers treat, what treatment approaches are utilized successfully, the extent of an athletic trainer's education, how athletic trainers are regulated, or the results of outcomes related to athletic training services.[10]

When dealing with third-party payers, one should believe the statement, "The meaning of communication is defined by the response it elicits."[17] A compiled list of suggestions for enhancing communication with nonclinician reviewers is found in Table 4-4.

FUTURE TRENDS IN CLAIMS FILING

One needs to stay abreast of the rapidly ongoing changes in health care to maintain a thorough understanding of how reimbursement will be affected. These changes can be seen at federal and state levels, and most importantly within the corporate business world of third-party payers. A provider who feels as though he or she is constantly playing "catch-up" with the rules of the game of reimbursement is probably on the right path to survival. By contrast, when a provider has a sense of understanding and stability with the reimbursement process, it is perhaps a strong sign that the particular individual is not aware of ongoing changes.

TOP 10 BILLING MISTAKES

1. Improper or incomplete documentation. Have a system in place to ensure you document and code for every service you provide. Only when services are clearly and completely listed with the appropriate diagnosis should charges be submitted to a carrier for payment.

2. Incomplete CPT code documentation. Document services in sufficient detail to support selected CPT codes. Incomplete documentation can result in denied charges, downcoded charges, extra staff time resubmitting claims, and increased risk of audit.

3. Incorrect levels of service. Improve your knowledge of different requirements for each level of service with respect to the type of history, exam, and complexity.

4. Omission of the fourth and fifth digits from ICD-9 (diagnosis) codes. Code to the highest level of specificity to reduce chances of a denied claim or delayed payment.

5. Nonspecific and incomplete diagnosis codes. Make sure diagnosis code symbols and abbreviations are correctly recognized and identified.

6. Assuming reimbursement procedures are uniform. Reimbursement policies are not the same from carrier to carrier. Read and understand each policy.

7. Failing to verify insurance coverage and precertification. Check for insurance coverage as well as for precertification procedures on all patients. Know the pre-certification requirements of your most often used managed care plans.

8. Lack of attention to detail. Know the little things, such as patient copay and deductible amounts, referral requirements, claim submission deadlines, etc. You will have fewer denials and more revenue.

9. Lack of analysis. Regularly review explanation of benefits (EOBs) statements for carrier payment policies, why denials are occurring, how quickly the office is getting paid, and whether fee adjustments are warranted.

10. Not knowing when or how to appeal a claim. Appeal all denied claims even if they were denied because of your mistake. A formal letter should accompany each claim appeal, as opposed to simply writing on the claim itself and sending it back.

One of the results of the current system of reimbursement is an abundance of paperwork. Clinicians have repeatedly expressed their concerns over losing quality time that could be spent with their patients but is instead used for paperwork purposes. This trend has also led to facilities hiring an increasingly larger number of administrative personnel. It is important to remember that the relationship between the clinicians and the administration may be the key to effective documentation and completeness of claims. Working together in a cohesive manner will allow for the facilitation of DPM.[18]

One attempt to reduce the paperwork trail has been in the form of electronic billing. Claims filed electronically appear to be the wave of the future. It has been estimated that nearly 25% of all submitted claims require additional documentation.[19] Electronic billing can reduce the cost of a claim between 25 to 50 cents each, which over a period of a year can demonstrate significant savings.[20] Furthermore, and unlike filing through the mail, electronic billing can be set up so that providers can receive confirmation reports from third-party payers upon receipt of each claim. The process of electronic billing has also been shown to significantly reduce the time between submission and response. Paper billing may take up to 4 months, whereas electronic billing may be completed in as short a time as 3 weeks.[21]

Electronic filing does not come without its share of drawbacks. To begin with, it can be quite expensive. Glassman reports that the total cost for appropriate hardware and software can be in excess of $45,000, excluding any additional maintenance or upgrade fees.[21] Relying solely on a computerized system may leave one susceptible to breakdowns and malfunctions. Thus, when a billing system undergoes failure, essentially all filing comes to a close until the problem is rectified. While electronic billing produces standardized documentation of skilled services, it may also lead to an exhibit whereby notes appear to be duplicative in nature, thus tremendously decreasing a clinician's individualized skills of thorough documentation and assessments.

Much of the future of claims filing will depend on how health care shapes itself in the next couple of years. The fight for dollars among health care providers and between health care providers and third-party payers will likely not become easier as we enter a new era of health care delivery. Regardless, the providers and the consumers must stand up for what they believe is correct and demand quality services. When a provider has an ample opportunity to deliver quality care to the point of patient satisfaction and good functional outcomes, perhaps all parties will then come to an agreement on a rational system for reimbursement. A system that runs efficiently and effectively will no doubt benefit all who utilize the services of claims filing.

REFERENCES

1. Konin JG. The basics of preparing and filing for reimbursement. Paper presented at: the 1998 National Athletic Trainers' Association Annual Symposium; June 17, 1998; Baltimore, Md.

2. Konin JG, Max J. Reimbursement and role delineation: what is it and who is qualified? *Ath Ther Today.* 1997;2(3):21-26.

3. American Medical Association. *Physician's Current Procedural Terminology.* Chicago, Ill: Author; 1998.

4. DeCarlo MS. Reimbursement for health care services. In: Konin JG, ed. *Clinical Athletic Training.* Thorofare, NJ: SLACK Incorporated; 1997.

5. Hayden D. American Medical Association Correspondence. October 21, 1996.

6. Practice Management Information Corp. *International Classification of Disease.* Los Angeles, Calif: Author; 1998.

7. Clifton DW, Tecklin JS. Under the watchful eye. *Rehab Management.* 1995;Dec/Jan:43-47.

8. Moffa-Trotter M, Anemaet WK. Writing goals for reimbursement. *Advance for Physical Therapists.* 1998;Jan 26:30.

9. Beckley NJ. Working with the finances. *Rehab Management.* 1996;April/May:101-103.

10. Abeln SH. Importance of documentation to patient care reimbursement. In: Stewart DL, Abeln SH, eds. *Documenting Functional Outcomes in Physical Therapy.* St. Louis, Mo: Mosby-Year Book; 1993:32-73.

11. Cohn R. Documentation guidelines for the E & M codes. *PT Magazine.* 1998;Jan:24-25.

12. Konin JG. Common mistakes in filing. *NATA News.* 1999;March:22.

13. American Physical Therapy Association. *Ask Your Reimbursement Expert.* www.apta.org. June 1998.

14. Ashby JJ. Denial process management. *Rehab Management.* 1997;Oct/Nov:82-83.

15. LePostollec M. Knowing the rules: communicating with utilization management organizations. *Advance for Physical Therapists.* 1998;March 2:46-47.

16. Wade J. Marketing to managed care payers. *Rehab Management.* 1996;June/July:111-113.

17. Lewis B, Pucelik F. *Magic Demystified: A Pragmatic Guide to Communication and Change.* Portland, Ore: Metamorphous Press; 1982.

18. Nosse LJ, Friberg DG. Reimbursement and documentation. In: Nosse LJ, Friberf DG, eds. *Management Principles for Physical Therapists.* Baltimore, Md: Williams & Wilkins; 1992.

19. Lansey D. Electronic claims submission. *PT Magazine.* 1998;March:24-26.

20. Rohland P. Filing and reimbursement in a flash. *Advance for Physical Therapists.* 1998;2:11-12.

21. Glassman S. Push button billing. *Advance for Physical Therapists.* 1998;3:11-13.

Chapter Five

Reimbursement for Athletic Trainers by Practice Setting

OBJECTIVES

Following the completion of this chapter, the reader will be able to:
- Identify and define the basic methods of provider reimbursement.
- Identify the different models of reimbursement for athletic trainers found in various athletic training practice settings.
- Identify the key requirements needed to establish an effective billing system for athletic trainers in the traditional setting.
- Define the athletic training reimbursement strategies that may be pursued at the secondary level.
- Define the types of reimbursement contracts that may be established in the industrial setting for athletic trainers.

REIMBURSING PROVIDERS

Today's health care system has a complex payment system for reimbursing providers. Historically, health care services have been provided under retrospective payment (after the services have been provided). This led to rapidly increasing costs as provider fees escalated. Prospective payment is much more common today. Under this system, payers have become increasingly involved in setting limits, rates, and methods by which they will reimburse providers before the service is provided.

Four basic reimbursement methods commonly used today are:
1. Fee-for-service—Direct payment for services rendered at the time of service. This fee schedule is based on usual, customary, and reasonable (UCR) charges.
2. Per visit reimbursement—The provider is reimbursed a specific amount each time a patient is treated. This is not as dependent on the specific services provided as in the fee-for-service reimbursement.
3. Per episode payment—Providers are given one payment for each episode or hospital admission, often by the diagnosis for which a patient requires medical intervention. This method bundles services into one payment and is based on the diagnosis.
4. Capitation—The form of reimbursement least related to services provided. With capitation, one payment for each health plan member is paid each month regardless of the utilization of services by that member. This is also sometimes referred to as per member per month (PMPM) payment system.

ATHLETIC TRAINING REIMBURSEMENT

Athletic training is reimbursed in a variety of ways, depending on the payer, type of services provided, and the site at which services were provided. The determination of which method of reimbursement is instituted typically is made by the payer when payer contracts are negotiated. It is important that athletic trainers be involved in these negotiations to identify services provided and enable payer recognition for athletic training services. Because athletic trainers do not have their own provider number (making them a recognizable entity for payers), this involvement is essential to achieving reimbursement. A capitated payment for athletic training services seems to be a logical and popular method of payment for the type of care provided by certified athletic trainers.

Following is a list of settings in which athletic trainers are typically employed.

Traditional athletic trainer settings:
- High school
- College/university
- Professional

Private practice settings:
- Certified outpatient rehabilitation facilities (CORFs)
- Therapist-owned rehabilitation practice other than CORFs
- Physician-owned rehabilitation practice other than CORFs
- Hospital settings
- Onsite outpatient rehabilitation
- Offsite outpatient satellite facilities
- High school outreach programs
- Onsite industrial rehabilitation
- Contracted from outside rehabilitation agency
- Works directly for the company
- High school outreach program (physician- or therapist-owned clinic)

Athletic training licensure acts impact services rendered and the ability to bill for those services in each of the settings listed above. At all times, the statutes listed in the athletic trainer licensure act for each individual state must be followed. Services billed must be billed as being done by an athletic trainer and not by any other allied health professional (ie, physical therapist, occupational therapist, or speech therapist).

REIMBURSEMENT IN THE CLINICAL SETTING

Shortly after sports medicine clinics began to evolve in the American health care system, athletic trainers were employed by the clinics to bring their expertise to the recreational athlete and to the physically active general public. Very soon after that, when clinics began to provide athletic training outreach services, it also became apparent that reimbursement of athletic training services would soon become imperative. Without reimbursement, athletic training was seen as a cost center. The possibility of reimbursement in the clinical setting for athletic training services surfaced in 1989. At that time, the state of Massachusetts passed a law that allowed licensed athletic trainers to receive reimbursement directly for services rendered.[1] The list of potential payers included schools, athletic associations, and insurance companies. There were restrictions built into the law, most notably the necessity of a physician referral. Despite the promise of reimbursement through legislative action, licensed athletic trainers in Massachusetts were not able to convince insurance companies to uniformly pay for services provided.

In the early 1990s, the Governmental Affairs Committee of the National Athletic Trainers' Association (NATA) approached the NATA Board of Directors to investigate the issue of reimbursement. The Reimbursement Advisory Group (RAG) was formed in 1995 under the aegis of the Governmental Affairs Committee. Almost immediately, the RAG began to hear of isolated instances where athletic trainers in clinical settings in states that regulated the profession were receiving a fee-for-service from third-party payers. These states included Ohio, Georgia, and Missouri. However, on further investigation, no pattern of uniformity of reimbursement was apparent.

It was not until 1993, when the state of Missouri allowed athletic training services to be part of the state employees' benefit package, that reimbursement became a reality. The history of success in obtaining reimbursement in Missouri began in 1986. Southwest Missouri State University converted its athletic training room into a sports medicine clinic and began receiving payment for services from insurance companies. Later, Ron Dunn, ATC/R, and Pat Forbis, ATC/R, from the Capitol Region Sports Medicine Clinic, convinced the state benefits plan manager that athletic training services provided for state employees and their dependents merited reimbursement. The campaign of Dunn and Forbis for acceptance of athletic training services as reimbursable services served as the blueprint for the RAG's *Approach to Payers Packet*.[2] Since that time, reports of reimbursement for athletic training services has been received by the RAG from these payers:

- Alliance Blue Cross
- Humana HMO-PPO
- United Health Care Select and Choice Plans
- Partners HMO-PPO
- Prudential Insurance Company
- First Health
- Champus
- John Alden Insurance
- Federated Insurance

APPROACHING PAYERS

The RAG, following the model suggested by Dunn and Forbis, compiled a collection of materials that could be duplicated by state athletic training associations to aid in approaching payers.[2] These materials later evolved into the RAG *Guide to Reimbursement* and are detailed in Chapter 3.

Additional suggestions by Dunn and Forbis included researching the major third-party payers in the state to determine the individuals who would make the decision on whether or not to reimburse athletic training services, exploring the use of outcomes data, and developing public relations campaigns. A critical point made by the RAG was that efforts to approach payers should be done in a concerted fashion through the state athletic training organization, rather than by individual clinics or athletic trainers. A piecemeal approach could have led to bidding wars among various clinics, engineered by payers, which would have been detrimental to the overall goal of acceptance of athletic training as a health profession. As outlays for health care continued to rise and subsequent reluctance of third-party payers to allow a newer allied health care profession into the reimbursement circle, other means of generating revenue for athletic training services would become necessary.

CLINICAL OUTREACH SERVICES

As noted earlier, sports medicine clinics began offering local high schools and small colleges the opportunity to contract for athletic training services in the early 1980s.[3] Outreach services could be provided in a range of visits including daily, twice weekly, weekly, or on an on-call basis. Revenue from contract fees and from event coverage fees (if not included in the contract language) posed partial relief of the cost of the outreach program. In addition, tracking of the athletes referred into the parent sports medicine clinic allowed for use of indirect revenues to help justify the outreach program. Many sports medicine clinics realized that the value of the outreach service lay in the community goodwill created by the presence of the athletic trainer within the school system. But local competition among sports medicine clinics for the contracts led to price wars where, within a given geographical area, outreach services ended up becoming a free service. To further help recover the cost of outreach athletic training services, athletic trainers employed in the clinical setting would often assist physical therapists during the time of day when the athletic trainers were not at the high school or college. This particular trend of athletic trainers being utilized in physical therapy clinics has raised its own set of concerns in relation to specific roles and responsibilities.

BILLING FOR ATHLETIC TRAINING SERVICES IN THE CLINICAL SETTING

There are several different settings in which an athletic trainer can be employed in private practice rehabilitation. A CORF is a private rehabilitation practice that has met federal Medicare guidelines and is certified by the Health Care Financing Administration (HCFA) as a Medicare provider. With Medicare being a federal program, individual state licenses do not affect it, as only federally recognized providers (eg, physical therapy, occupational therapy, speech therapy, etc) are able to treat patients in this setting. The athletic trainer employed in this setting usually functions under the supervision of a Medicare-approved provider and may not bill for services provided to Medicare patients. Certified athletic trainers may treat non-Medicare patients in a CORF, and reimbursement by commercial payers can be expected.

In privately owned rehabilitation clinics not designated as CORFs there is significantly more professional freedom for the licensed athletic trainer, much of which depends on the treatment and professional philosophy of the owner(s) and other allied health professionals employed by the facility. Care must be exercised to practice within the state athletic training regulatory act. An athletic trainer may not perform patient evaluations or treatment and bill it as a physical therapist (ie, that is, acting as a physical therapist, which is not within the license of an athletic trainer). Make sure a thorough knowledge exists regarding what certified athletic trainers are legally permitted to do. A thorough understanding of the physical therapy practice act is also critical to prevent misinterpretations and misunderstanding.

Physician-owned rehabilitation clinics provide the option of treating patients using the physician's provider number. This type of treatment setting, working under the direction of a physician, gives the athletic trainer significant professional freedom to practice athletic training. The athletic trainer must prove to the physician what services he or she is capable of performing, with the physician being confident enough in the athletic trainer to provide the quality of services which that particular physician expects.

In a hospital setting, the athletic trainer must work within the guidelines established by that particular hospital. Reference should be made to the hospital billing code for athletic training services, UB Code 95x1, and the scope of practice outlined in state athletic training regulatory acts to substantiate services provided by certified athletic trainers in hospital settings.

There is increasing evidence of third-party reimbursement occurring for athletic trainers acting as physician extenders in the clinical setting. Evaluation and re-evaluation, therapeutic exercise instruction to patients, and brace/support fitting in conjunction with the physician visit may be billed utilizing the appropriate current procedural terminology (CPT) code (physical medicine series) and physician provider numbers. In some cases, physician provider numbers may not be needed, depending on the payer. The role of the athletic trainer as a physician extender is definitely an identity that is actively being pursued and developed, as it best fits the educational preparation and function model of an athletic trainer. This role takes the athletic trainer out of the typical clinical domain of the physical therapist and puts him or her in a position to exercise his or her skills in clinical decision making and provide a wide range of services to clients under the direction of a physician. This model is being promoted through an educational campaign developed by the NATA RAG, directed at payers.

CAVEATS OF CLINICAL ATHLETIC TRAINING

As athletic trainers enter into the reimbursement realm, several major caveats await them. Among them are:

- Knowledge of the state athletic training practice act
- Competition with other allied health care providers
- Recognition by third-party payers
- The ethics of earning a fee-for-service

Athletic training has long been a nonrevenue-generating profession, and the intricacies of the laws associated with revenue generation are an entirely new area for athletic trainers. Athletic trainers are cautioned to thoroughly explore all aspects of pursuing reimbursement to make certain that legal and ethical guidelines are followed.

State Athletic Practice Acts

The regulations that govern the practice of athletic training differ from state to state. It is crucial that each athletic trainer know the athletic training regulation of his or her state. Some states restrict the type of athlete/patient that an athletic trainer may treat. Some states restrict the setting in which an athletic trainer may treat athletes or patients. Some states restrict the types of modalities that athletic trainers may use in treatment or may restrict the body part being treated.[4] Athletic trainers are advised to know which activities are allowed by their individual state regulations, as well as those activities that are prohibited by these statutes.

Overlap with Physical Therapy

Since elements of athletic training are found within the scope of practice of physical therapy, athletic trainers must present their services as athletic training services, not as physical therapy services. To do so otherwise would be fraudulent.

Business Ethics

Athletic trainers are well aware of the ethics of being an allied health care professional. Acting in the best interest of the athlete or patient, not harming the athlete or patient, and fully informing the athlete or patient of the purpose of treatment and of other treatment options available are common practice standards for athletic trainers. In the reimbursement arena, however, other areas of knowledge are equally important. Understanding the need for "arm's length" from a referral source, what constitutes a "safe harbor," or what are illegal billing practices are among many issues that clinical athletic trainers need to understand for the future. The RAG appears to be the agency of the NATA that will educate athletic trainers on these issues until such time that the educators of athletic training curriculums develop appropriate courses. Athletic trainers who are in the clinical setting are urged to seek out other sources of information as well.

Future of Reimbursement in Clinical Athletic Training

Reimbursement for athletic training services appears to be steadily increasing.[5,6] It is difficult to say when universal reimbursement of athletic training services will occur. Key components toward that end appear to be acceptance of athletic trainers as reimbursable health care professionals by the federal government (see Chapter Three), regulation of athletic training by all states, and realization by third-party payers that athletic trainers bring a unique set of skills and techniques coupled with a recognized knowledge base to health care. Paramount in this last component is the recognition by third-party payers that their customers are demanding this type of health care. Perhaps this is the criterion for reimbursement: when public demand for athletic training services reaches the point which is fiscally more advantageous for an insurance company to pay out than to lose revenue from premiums when customers leave to seek payers who will reimburse for athletic training services.

ATHLETIC TRAINING REIMBURSEMENT IN THE TRADITIONAL SETTING

Models of reimbursement for athletic trainers in the traditional setting have been and continue to be explored. The creation of revenue centers in traditional athletic training settings could be a major factor in securing and maintaining athletic training positions at the college and university level as well as at the secondary level. Objectively demonstrating the value of certified athletic trainers will help protect jobs from takeover by for-profit companies able to demonstrate income by billing for rehabilitation services.

There are two important questions that arise when considering billing in the traditional setting:
1. Is it appropriate to bill for services rendered in this setting? This addresses professional philosophy as well as the philosophy of the institution.
2. Will third-party payers recognize the services provided and reimburse for these billed services?

REIMBURSEMENT MODELS

Evidence of reimbursement for athletic training services in the collegiate setting can be traced to the early 1980s. Ivan Milton, ATC, director of Athletic Training Services at Southwest Missouri State University, began billing outpatient services from the athletic training room in 1982.[7] Patients were primarily from area secondary schools. Billing for these outpatient services moved to another campus location in 1986, and a subsequent partnership with a local hospital resulted in its location being moved to the hospital campus. Billing for university athletes in the training room, specifically for postoperative rehabilitation, began in 1991. This was expanded to billing for all time-loss injury rehabilitation in 1993.

The Missouri State Athletic Trainer Practice Act defines the scope of practice for athletic trainers in Missouri and provides the framework for establishing a system of reimbursement for licensed/certified athletic trainers. Legal council and university administration were consulted throughout the development of the program. Treatment protocols were developed, approved, and signed by team and consulting physicians (Figure 5-1).[7]

An electronic billing system was implemented to facilitate claims filing, and secretarial support was added to manage all billing functions. Medical practice management software with rehabilitation/therapy reporting options was also utilized to assist in the claims processing function. Typical software packages allow easy access to patient information, administrative/financial information, and operational data. Table 5-1 provides a sample list of detailed reports generated by standard software.[7]

MISSOURI ATHLETIC TRAINER
REGISTRATION FUNCTIONAL PROTOCOL

_____, ATC _____

Institution

I, _____, MD, as team physician/consulting physician, hereby authorize the above named person to act on my behalf during my absence. Such authority shall include the following area(s) I have initialed:

___Evaluation

___Emergency Care

___First Aid and Treatment

___Transportation and Evacuation

___Preventive and Protective Measures

___Muscle and Joint Testing and Evaluation

___Administration of Rehabilitation Programs

___Supervision of Conditioning Programs

___Application of Compression Wraps, Casts, Splints

___Appliances, and Devices

___Application of Physical Modalities such as Heat, Cold, Air, Water, Electricity, Sound, and Light

___Education and Counsel on Health Care Information

In addition, I authorize the following:

_____, ATC will assist or carry out any other instructions or procedures I feel warranted or necessary to effect care, rehabilitation, or both.

_____

Athletic Trainer Signature/Date

_____

Team or Consulting Physician Signature/Date

Figure 5-1. Missouri athletic trainer registration functional protocol.

Table 5-1

REPORTS

Reports that Tell About Patients

- Patient names and addresses
- Patients who were referred by other professionals
- Patient balances
- Patient birthdays, by month
- Inactive patients
- Patients with a specific diagnosis
- Objective diagnosis history
- Patients and diagnoses

Reports to Give Patients

- Patient charge slip (receipt)
- Patient statements
- Superstatements
- Detailed patient ledger
- Individual patient budget plan

Reports that Tell About Practice

- Production report
- Audit report
- Practice statistics
- CPT group summary daysheet
- Year-end report series

Reports to Help Track Practice Finances

- Carrier balances
- Receivables
- Budget plans list
- Patient statement register
- Charges by date of service
- Payments by date of deposit
- Payment history
- Charges history

Table 5-1 continued

Reports to Control Day-to-Day Activities

- Appointment lists
- Patients due for recalls
- Daily receipts and deposits
- Daily patient summary
- New patient registration form
- Management care and capitation fee comparison

Support for Insurance Collection Efforts

- Insurance carrier data audit
- HCFA-1500 claim form
- UB-92 claim form
- Insurance ledger
- Insurance claim tracer

Word Processing and Report Writing Capabilities

- Personalized letter
- Personalized reports
- Labels

Computer System Reports

- System set-up choices
- Diagnoses list
- Insurance carriers list
- Provider list
- Procedures list
- Referring physicians list
- Facilities list

Information regarding athletic insurance claims procedures is provided to parents of student athletes (Figure 5-2)[7] and appropriate medical releases are obtained. Injury/condition evaluations follow standard SOAP note format. Specific ICD-9 (International Classification of Diseases diagnoses) codes are utilized along with CPT codes designating services/treatment provided. Frequently utilized routine techniques of athletic training, such as prophylactic taping and icing, are not billed.

To: The Parent of _____

Intercollegiate Athletes

We are extremely pleased to have your son/daughter as a student athlete at _____ and hope that he/she will achiever academic, social, and athletic success.

Each student athlete is required to have a medical history questionnaire on file and complete a physical examination prior to participation in any collegiate sport. The final decision on physical qualifications or reason for rejection is the responsibility of the team physician and athletic trainer. The team physician and athletic trainer also make the decision on if or when an athlete may return to competition after an injury.

Accidents do occur and we attempt to provide our athletes with the very best possible care. Medical bills may be incurred when the athlete is treated for bodily injury due to an accident, whether locally, during a road trip, or by a medical vendor in his/her own home area.

The NCAA discourages any university from providing coverage or paying the bills incurred for expenses related to illnesses or conditions that are not sustained as the direct result of an accident in our intercollegiate sports program (this includes pre-existing conditions and nonathletic injuries).

The athletic accident insurance at _____ provides coverage for your son/daughter for accidents while participating in the play or official team practice of intercollegiate sports, including sponsored and authorized team travel.

Claim Procedures

All medical bills for your son/daughter that were incurred as the result of an accident in the intercollegiate sports program will be sent directly to your son/daughter or to your home address. In some cases, the athletic department may receive a copy of the bill, but in no case will the athletic department be the primary place for the incurred bill to be sent.

1. Send to: Athletic Training Services; _____, a copy of all bills and all insurance responses.

2. Submit the bills incurred to your family employer group or plan first. They will do one of two things:

   A. Accept the claim and pay all or a portion of the bills incurred. An explanation of benefits (EOB) will be mailed to you; please forward a copy of this to Athletic Training Services.

   B. Reject the claim and send you a letter of denial. An example might be that your son/daughter is no longer part of your group policy after reaching the age of 23. Send a copy of this to Athletic Training Services.

Figure 5-2. Sample letter describing athletic insurance claims procedures, provided to parents of student athletes.

<table>
<tr><td>3.</td><td>If a balance remains after your family employer group insurance or plan administrator, send the letter of denial and a copy of the bills incurred to Athletic Training Services.

If you receive a letter of denial from your family employer group insurance or plan administrator, send the letter of denial and a copy of the bills incurred to Athletic Training Services. If no coverage is available, a letter from your employer with verification will be necessary.</td></tr>
<tr><td>4.</td><td>If the bills incurred are not paid by the family employer group insurance or plan, the claim will be sent from the athletic department to our insurance carrier's office for processing. If they need any additional information, please cooperate with them and they will process the claim in the least possible amount of time. It is in your best interest to have the claim settled promptly since all the bills incurred are in your name.</td></tr>
</table>

Please note: If the primary family coverage is through an HMO (health maintenance organization), you must follow the proper procedures required by your plan in order for the university's insurance to satisfactorily complete its portion of the claim. This is especially important if your plan requires preauthorization to have your son/daughter treated if out of your plan's service area.

You should retain this letter for future reference. Your cooperation in this important area will help make this program successful in minimizing delays and accomplishing the purpose for which it is intended.

Figure 5-2. Continued.

Treatment guidelines are established and followed. Treatment plans are established with specific treatment protocols including corresponding CPT codes. Itemized statements are prepared and claims are filed with appropriate payers (Figure 5-3).[7] If parents are filing the claim, appropriate instructions are sent to them regarding filing preparation and documentation. Reimbursement is provided by the payer directly to athletic training services.

VARIATIONS OF COLLEGIATE REIMBURSEMENT MODELS

Other existing models of reimbursement for athletic trainers at the collegiate level involve a partnership with physical therapists. The sports medicine department at Georgia Tech University, then under the direction of Jay Shoop, MA, ATC/L, initiated a billing process for athlete health care occurring in the training room for services provided by physical therapists and athletic trainers. Physical therapists cosign treatments provided by certified athletic trainers. Revenue generated is paid directly to the sports medicine department.

Still other models utilize athletic trainers in student health centers to provide treatments for athletes, the general student body, and faculty (sometimes including family) and staff. In some instances, athletic trainers are the sole providers or may provide services in combination with physical therapists or other related allied health care personnel. State athletic training regulatory acts often dictate which model is appropriate.

Table 5-2 illustrates issues to examine when considering implementing third-party billing in a college or university setting.[9]

ITEMIZED STATEMENT

PATIENT: DATE:

                                                 IRS#: 00-0000000

SS#:   POL#:   EMPLOYER: STUDENT-FB
DATE/INJ: GRP#:
TO:

DIAGNOSIS:
844.2 ACL TEAR (ACUTE)
717.4 LATERAL MENISCUS DERANGEMENT

FC: COMM-INS
DATE OF LAST BILL: / /

DATE	CPT	DESCRIPTION	*POS TOS	#	AMOUNT
08/12/96	97010	Hydrocollator/Cryotherapy	11	1	25.00
08/12/96	99070	Established Patient Extensive Service	11	1	25.00
08/12/96	73560	Knee 3 Views	11	1	25.00
08/12/96	99070	Elastice Wrap	11	1	5.00
08/12/96	99070	Knee Orthosis Rehab	11	1	175.00
08/12/96	97010.9	Crutch rental 1 Month Minimum	11	1	35.00
08/13/96	97010	Hydrocollator/Cryotherapy	11	1	25.00
08/13/96	97110	Therapeutic Exercises	11	1	30.00
08/15/96	97010	Hydrocollator/Cryotherapy	11	1	25.00
08/14/96	97110	Therapeutic Exercises	11	1	30.00
08/15/96	99071	Exercise Procedural Manual	11	1	10.00
08/17/96	97799	Back to School Education/Family Confer./H	11	1	25.00
08/23/96	97010	Hydrocollator/Cryotherapy	11	1	25.00
08/23/96	97110	Therapeutic Exercises	11	1	30.00
08/25/96	97010	Hydrocollator/Cryotherapy	11	1	25.00
08/25/96	97110	Therapeutic Exercises	11	1	30.00
08/26/96	97010	Hydrocollator/Cryotherapy	11	1	25.00
08/26/96	97110	Therapeutic Exercises	11	1	30.00
08/27/96	97010	Hydrocollator/Cryotherapy	11	1	25.00
08/27/96	97118	Electric Stimulation	11	1	25.00
08/27/96	97110	Therapeutic Exercises	11	1	30.00
08/28/96	97010	Hydrocollator/Cryotherapy	11	1	25.00
08/28/96	97118	Electric Stimulation	11	1	25.00
08/28/96	97110	Therapeutic Exercises	11	1	30.00
08/29/96	97010	Hydrocollator/Cryotherapy	11	1	25.00
		CONTINUED			

SUBTOTAL: 785.00
Page   1

Figure 5-3. Itemized statement.

ITEMIZED STATEMENT

DATE	CPT	DESCRIPTION	*POS TOS	#	AMOUNT
08/29/96	97118	Electric Stimulation	11	1	25.00
08/29/96	97110	Therapeutic Exercises	11	1	30.00
08/30/96	97010	Hydrocollator/Cryotherapy	11	1	25.00
08/30/96	97118	Electric Stimulation	11	1	25.00
08/30/96	97110	Therapeutic Exercises	11	1	30.00

PROVIDER:
TOTAL: $920.00

Page   2

Figure 5-3. Continued.

BILLING FOR SOFT GOODS

Some athletic training programs choose to bill for soft goods only or may use this as a first step in initiating a full scale reimbursement system for athletic training services. Items such as ankle braces, knee braces, shoulder braces, and other supportive devices, if physician prescribed for a specific condition/diagnosis, can and should be reimbursed by insurance. Sports medicine and/or athletic departments should not have to incur expenses associated with providing these materials.

BILLING AT THE SECONDARY SCHOOL LEVEL

Few models of reimbursement for athletic training services currently exist at the secondary school level. However, the same basic principles of reimbursement can be applied to that setting.

Athletic trainers can carry out prescribed postsurgical rehabilitation and bill the individual's insurance through the attending physician's office management/billing system. Soft goods may be able to be directly billed. It may even be possible to create a revenue center for a high school athletic program similar to those models at the collegiate level.

Some large high schools employ physical therapists and other allied health care professionals to manage the health care needs of their special education populations. In these instances, a system of medical billing or contracted medical services may already be in place, and athletic training services may easily be incorporated into that existing system.

Creatively exploring these issues with school administrations, legal council, and state athletic training reimbursement groups is the first step in addressing the development of reimbursement for athletic training services and creating a model reimbursement program at the secondary level.

Reimbursement for athletic training services at the collegiate and secondary school levels is in its infancy. Many different models and variations of those models will develop in the future. Reimbursement in these practice settings is not, however, for everyone. It will remain an option for those seeking creative ways to substantiate the value of their athletic training services and/or demonstrate ways to generate revenue contributing to job security and job development.

Reimbursement in these settings is another way to enhance the identity of the athletic trainer in the health care community and demonstrate the value of athletic training services.

Table 5-2

ISSUES TO CONSIDER WHEN BILLING IN A COLLEGE/UNIVERSITY SETTING

I. Billing

    A. Who bills?

       1. Solely done by ATC?

       2. Under the direction of a PT?

       3. Determining factors

          a. State laws

          b. Professional practice acts

          c. Insurance company's payment

    B. Who gets billed?

       1. Students, faculty, staff

       2. Outside patients

       3. Athletes

          a. Every athlete?

          b. Only athletes with long-term rehabilitation?

          c. If seen 5 days per week, are they billed 5 days per week?

II. Determining ownership

    A. College/university

    B. Athletic association/department

    C. Outside corporation

    D.   Private corporation

III. Allocation of funds

    A. Determined by ownership

IV. Other considerations

    A. Campus medical facility or student health center

       1. Rehabilitation services provided there?

    B. Support from key factors

       1. Campus medical community

       2. Team physicians

Table 5-2 continued
3. Local physicians
4. Coaches and administrators
V. Effects on the operation of the athletic training room and care of the student athletes

ATHLETIC TRAINING IN THE INDUSTRIAL SETTING

It is becoming increasingly common for corporations, in an attempt to reduce their workers' compensation costs, to consider developing an industrial athletic training program in their plants and facilities. Evidence of these programs was formally documented in the mid 1980s. An example was Walbro Corporation, a manufacturer of fuel system components and small engine carburetors in Michigan, who contracted Athletic Training Services, Inc. Athletic Training Services is a consulting firm that specializes in inhouse health maintenance, prevention, and rehabilitation programs, utilizing certified athletic trainers, to develop such a program in their plants. Other in-house rehabilitation programs utilizing athletic trainers existed before that time in selected corporations throughout the country, but the Walbro model was the most comprehensive and created national exposure for the concept. Cost savings were emphasized and much interest was generated throughout the corporate community.

Statistics have shown that minor sprains, strains, and common overuse conditions account for more than 75% of reported workplace injuries. Workplace health and safety is an increasing concern of the Occupational Safety and Health Administration (OSHA). It is estimated that more than 650,000 workers suffer job-related injuries each year, costing employers up to 20 billion dollars a year in workers' compensation claims. OSHA is emphasizing regulations to help reduce workplace injuries and identify and assess hazards to which employees are exposed. Requirements are being instituted that mandate employers develop programs to help workers avoid injuries resulting from heavy lifting and repetitive motion activities. The recognition of musculoskeletal disorders in the workplace is finally being realized, and efforts are being made to implement preventative measures. With this emphasis, industrial athletic training programs could receive a great deal of impetus.

Reducing these injuries and/or the time it takes to recover from them can have a significant financial impact on a company. An analysis of previous workers' compensation claims can identify injury patterns and related costs for a corporation, providing information to develop a plan of intervention utilizing certified athletic trainers as the provider. An inhouse rehabilitation program for all employees, staffed by certified athletic trainers and supervised by plant physicians and/or consulting occupational medicine physicians in consultation and cooperation with management, has been shown to produce effective, cost-saving results. Through a well-planned program of prevention, of specific task-related ergonomic analyses, treatment, and rehabilitation, many programs project a minimum 25% reduction in workers' compensation costs, as well as a significant decrease in employee absentee rates.

In addition, industrial athletic trainers may be utilized to develop and supervise onsite health employee and fitness programs. Emphasizing wellness and prevention, these programs typically focus on cardiovascular and resistance training along with health promotion interventions, such as weight management and smoking cessation programs. These health and fitness programs are also often available to employees' families.

An inhouse rehabilitation clinic provides employees with the convenience of seeking injury assessment and treatment onsite when the injury occurs. It provides flexibility in terms of scheduling appointments and allows the employee to visit the clinic between work shifts and at scheduled breaks.

Table 5-3

INDUSTRIAL ATHLETIC TRAINING

Advantages to Employers

- Concept of injury prevention is introduced into the workplace, potentially reducing costs.
- Employees receive prompt treatment for injuries, reducing lost time.
- Demonstrates company commitment to employee health, improving morale.
- Encourages employees to lead healthy lifestyles, improving productivity.
- Employees exercise to help reduce stress, improving health and productivity.
- Reduces workers' compensation costs, improving profitability.
- Reduces sick days per year, improving productivity.
- Better ergonomics are introduced to employees, improving quality control and preventing injury.

Light duty programs, designed to modify work assignments in relation to injury, can be supervised and monitored by the inhouse athletic training staff. Having the clinic onsite also encourages employees to utilize the service as an information, advice, and educational resource. Educational materials can be made available free of charge and individual questions can be directly answered. A partnership is developed between the health care providers, employees, and management demonstrating that the employer is supporting the workers throughout their injury prevention and rehabilitation by providing quality care inhouse.

Industrial athletic training programs have increased in popularity and many major corporations such as General Motors, General Electric, and the Tennessee Valley Authority have incorporated industrial athletic training programs in their plants and corporate facilities. The advantages to employers are becoming increasingly evident (Table 5-3).

BILLING FOR ATHLETIC TRAINING
SERVICES IN THE INDUSTRIAL SETTING

All referrals to athletic trainers in the industrial setting come directly from physicians. This may be the plant physician(s) or consulting physicians. Specific treatment protocols are developed by physicians and carried out by the certified athletic trainer.

Athletic training services can be reimbursed in industry in a variety of ways. These include:
- Flat fee
- Hourly rate
- Fee-for-service
- Profit sharing

In a contract based on flat fee-for-service, athletic training services are provided for a predetermined amount. The fee is determined by the amount of staff and equipment needed and workers' compensa-

Table 5-4

WHY SHOULD CERTIFIED ATHLETIC TRAINERS BE IN THE INDUSTRIAL WORKPLACE?

- Prevention of potential injuries.
- Early recognition and treatment of musculoskeletal injuries
- Safe, expedient return to work
- Effective injury management

tion claim history. The length of contract is negotiable and a partnership approach is emphasized in determining fees and services provided. A flat fee-for-service system is beneficial for both parties to decrease the overall number of cases and length of treatment. It is easier for the client to budget and the amount of future expenses can easily be determined.

Hourly rate for services involves a flat fee per hour while onsite providing care. The rate depends on the amount of staff and equipment needed. Expenses vary depending on the hours spent onsite. This system provides coverage for overtime if needed. If less than 40 hours per week are needed, the client realizes a benefit in savings. The hourly rate for service system is more difficult for the client to budget and more difficult for future expenses to be projected.

The fee-for-service reimbursement system involves payment for each service provided. The fee is determined by staff and equipment needed and projections as to the amount of services to be delivered. Costs vary depending on the number of services provided in a given period of time. This system presents some difficulty for clients in relation to budgeting and projecting future expenses.

Profit sharing involves a fee for current cost with no profit margin incorporated. The rate depends on staff and equipment needed and can be determined by records of previous workers' compensation claims, including days lost and expenses. The profit sharing system provides incentive to decrease the number of injury cases. It is easy for the client to budget and payment depends on performance. Valid measurable data must be available to compare current expenditures with previous expenditures. The amount of profit must be negotiated so that it is flexible with changes in the work environment such as overtime, increased number of employees, etc.

Though examples of all of these models exist throughout industry, the most common at this time involves the flat fee-for-service reimbursement model executed through specific, individualized contracts, often incorporating guarantees and incentives. Guarantees are often based on projected savings based on previous claim history and workers' compensation expenses. Incentives are usually based on exceeding projected goals. A continuing evolution of these models will be seen in the future and innovative approaches will develop from them.

CONCLUSION

It is becoming increasingly evident that certified athletic trainers are extremely valuable providers in the industrial workplace providing injury prevention, early recognition and treatment of musculoskeletal injuries, expediting a safe and prompt return to work, and developing an overall effective and cost-saving injury management program (Table 5-4). Certified athletic trainers are an important part of the industrial health care team and provide services that benefit industry and employees.

REFERENCES

1. Hunt V. Revised law permits ATCs in Massachusetts to bill for services. *NATA News.* 1989;2:6.

2. National Athletic Trainers' Association, Office of Governmental Relations. *Approach to Payers Packet.* Dallas, Tex: NATA; 1996.

3. Sherman B. A new approach to athletic training in southern Wisconsin high schools. *The Physician and Sportsmedicine.* 1985;13:57-64.

4. Konin J, ed. *Clinical Athletic Training.* Thorofare, NJ: SLACK Incorporated; 1997.

5. Hunt V. Reimbursement group sees progress as key for future development. *NATA News.* 1998;2:10-13.

6. Hunt V. Will campus clinics replace traditional training rooms? *NATA News.* 1990;3:2.

7. Milton I. *Athletic Trainer Reimbursement in the Traditional Setting.* Springfield, Mo: Southwest Missouri State University; 1997.

8. Shoop JL. Outline of a billing strategy: billing in universities complex. *NATA News.* 1999;May.

Chapter Six

Reimbursement Strategies

OBJECTIVES

Following the completion of this chapter the reader will be able to:
- Identify the key strategies for achieving reimbursement.
- Discuss and demonstrate the creative use of outcomes data.
- Identify and effectively develop physician alliances and client support to further reimbursement efforts.
- Understand legislative efforts needed to pursue Medicare recognition.

In the ever-changing world of health care, strategies for achieving reimbursement must continually be reassessed and will change rapidly and frequently. Strategies are dictated by changes in payer provisions and government health care agency reimbursement policies. These changes must be closely monitored, and there must be a constant awareness of reimbursement trends and anticipated policy changes. Strategies, to be effective, must be proactive in nature, anticipating future trends and policies rather than reacting to them once they are in place.

PAYER RECOGNITION

The primary determinant in achieving reimbursement is payer recognition. Payers must recognize and approve the provider of services before reimbursement can be approved. Standardized treatment and facility codes specific to athletic training greatly assist in establishing this identity, however, educating payers regarding the effectiveness and value of services provided by certified athletic trainers is the key.

Typically, insurance company policy is made on a state level. Although national company policy is established in some areas, the individual state carriers are usually primarily responsible for the final say in provider recognition issues. Having athletic training included in contract language is a state level decision. Therefore, lobbying efforts directed at payers must be organized by state, first identifying the primary carriers in each state and then researching payer history in relation to physical medicine services and recognition of new providers. Following that analysis, a specific strategic plan needs to be developed and implemented in regard to approaching payers for athletic training recognition (see Chapter Three). Often times, when payers in individual states create policy, it is easier to convince the same company in other states to do the same.

Evidence must be presented that clearly demonstrates the effectiveness and value of athletic training. Payers must be convinced that athletic training is a service that is not represented by other health care providers. The model of the athletic trainer as physician extender can effectively demonstrate that difference.

Efforts to accomplish the same goal continue at the national level with major health insurance companies. The combination of these efforts at the national and state levels will prove to have the greatest impact.

REIMBURSEMENT EVIDENCE

One of the most effective reimbursement strategies is presenting current evidence of athletic training reimbursement. Often times this evidence will create a domino effect with other payers. Evidence of reimbursement for athletic training services exists throughout the country. Determining which payers in individual states are reimbursing for athletic training services and using that evidence when approaching additional payers can be very effective.

National managed care organizations and government health care agencies do set national policy. Evidence of reimbursement also becomes meaningful to them as they consider future policy changes. Efforts should be continually made to track evidence of reimbursement in local and state areas to further support and substantiate this strategy.

CREATIVE USE OF OUTCOMES DATA

Outcomes data can be an extremely effective tool in developing reimbursement strategies. Although it has been difficult to quantify the exact effect of outcomes data on improving reimbursement status among providers, it has been demonstrated that payers are extremely cognizant of the value of this information and the attention to quality assurance and a high a standard of patient care that it represents. Outcomes data have influenced practice guidelines, treatment protocols, and reimbursement patterns of high volume, high-cost medical interventions such as coronary artery bypass surgery, spine surgery, and total joint replacement surgery. Based on the use of outcomes data for this decision making, the future looks bright for continued and expanded reliance on this type of information for future decision making.

Outcomes data can be utilized for internal or external purposes. Internal uses can include intrapractice provider comparisons, internal quality assurance assessments, and the evaluation of clinical practice protocols. Specific to athletic training, outcomes data can be used internally to compare the result of treatment(s) provided by athletic trainers with other allied health care professionals within that practice. A cost-benefit analysis can be added to that comparison to demonstrate and express value.

Outcomes data become important for external audiences to validate the effectiveness of the athletic trainer as a valuable health care provider. Outcomes data documenting the effect of care provided by athletic trainers can be presented to payers as supporting evidence for including athletic trainers as approved, reimbursable providers. These strategies have and will continue to be employed with commercial payers as well as managed care organizations and government health care entities. In addition, outcomes data provide an explicit, standardized, nontechnical measure of effectiveness of care provided to patients, answering the basic question, "Did the patient get better as a result of treatment provided?" This provides support for new and/or nontraditional treatment techniques and protocols that otherwise may not have been considered or accepted.

Outcomes data can be extremely valuable in marketing efforts, using the all-important measure of patient satisfaction in describing services provided. Patient advocacy and support for preferred providers based on outcome and satisfaction has a definite influence on payers recognizing and reimbursing providers for specific treatment protocols. Outcomes data can also be used in marketing success rates and low complication rates of selected interventions.

Outcomes research results are an excellent means of creatively marketing a practice or profession. Specific research protocols addressing issues of patient outcome can be developed, focusing on specif-

Table 6-1
CREATIVE USE OF OUTCOMES DATA
• Compare to national benchmarks
• Compare to competitors' outcomes
• Demonstrate provider uniqueness
• Be proactive in approaching payers
• Show cost-benefit relationship

ic providers (ie, athletic trainers) providing specific treatment interventions. Resultant data can be effectively utilized to substantiate the effect of care provided by athletic trainers. Generating additional objective data regarding the effectiveness and efficiency of athletic training services is a strategy to pursue in gaining reimbursement identity. Research commonly referred to as demonstration projects are typically established to illustrate a specific point or outcome. If evidence is lacking in a particular area, a demonstration project can be initiated to provide data relative to a specific question. For instance, athletic trainers may not have historical evidence in care provided to a nonathletic population. A research project specifically evaluating outcomes with a specific population could serve to provide that data. However, it must be remembered that research projects may be costly and time-consuming. Often times the information is needed well before project data are available.

Outcomes data can also be utilized to compare outcomes between health care professionals. Several large national outcomes databases have data available from a variety of health care professions, which allow for comparative analyses. Such an analysis was conducted by Focus on Therapeutic Outcomes, Inc (FOTO) in 1999 comparing the outcomes of care provided by certified athletic trainers versus physical therapists in sports medicine clinic settings.[1] FOTO, Inc is a nationally known outcomes research management corporation specializing in outcomes research for the physical therapy profession. Results of that comparative analysis indicated that care provided by athletic trainers produces comparable outcomes, patient satisfaction, and value when compared to physical therapists. This type of information can be extremely valuable when marketing services provided by athletic trainers to payers, employers, and/or physician providers.

In addition, outcomes data can be utilized for peer review publication in scientific journals, contributing to the body of knowledge on the subject of outcomes research and effective medical interventions, validating the role of the certified athletic trainer as a scientific investigator. This contributes to further developing the identity of the athletic trainer in the health care community.

The role of outcomes data in developing creative reimbursement strategies is extremely important. The key to achieving reimbursement and establishing a position of importance as a health care provider is directly related to demonstrating value. Outcomes data will assist in quantitatively and qualitatively demonstrating that value (Table 6-1).

PHYSICIAN ALLIANCES

Athletic trainers have had long-standing relationships with sports medicine physicians. Working as a team, the athletic trainer and team physician develop close working relationships and share a high degree of mutual respect. Once almost exclusively maintained with orthopedic surgeons, these relationships have expanded to the variety of physician providers now found in the sports medicine arena. The athletic trainer is considered a valued, integral part of the health care team, providing care to physically active people.

These physician-athletic trainer relationships should be emphasized and maximized when developing reimbursement strategies. The voice of the physician definitely carries authority and can be very influential in establishing reimbursement identity and recognition for athletic trainers. Often times, physicians serve on managed care panels and can directly affect reimbursement policies for national managed care organizations. It is this type of input that can create a reimbursement policy for athletic training services and have athletic trainers recognized as providers. Although athletic trainers have difficulty being represented on these various medical panels, physicians who have worked with athletic trainers and recognize their value can certainly be influential in speaking on their behalf.

These physician-athletic trainer alliances must be developed on local, state, and national levels. Communication has been established on the national level with a variety of physician organizations directly related to sports medicine. This includes organizations that have membership in and participate in the activities of the Joint Commission on Sports Medicine and Science (Table 6-2). Establishing relationships with individual state medical associations and the sports medicine committees within those groups is an excellent place to start to further develop effective physician alliances.

CLIENT SUPPORT

Patients and clients who benefit from the services provided by health care providers have a very strong, effective voice in relation to their health care provisions. Historical evidence has clearly demonstrated that the voice of the people can change health care reimbursement patterns. Traditionally, the athletic trainer has been known for his or her effective interpersonal relationships with his or her clients, contributes to positive outcomes. Patient satisfaction with treatment provided by athletic trainers has been documented at more than 98%.[2] Patients should communicate their support of athletic trainers to payers to influence their decision making in relation to reimbursement practices. If the lives covered by health plans demand certain provisions and specific providers, and outcomes can substantiate their demands, payers will be forced to listen, and reimbursement patterns may change. Many current reimbursed health care professions have utilized this strategy in achieving reimbursement for their providers. Individual clients should be encouraged to communicate their preferences and opinions to their health care plan administrators. Efforts should be organized and coordinated to create a unified approach in relation to this strategy.

LEGISLATIVE EFFORTS

Medicare

Legislation to effect changes in Medicare reimbursement policies to include athletic training services is being pursued at the national level. This process can be lengthy and affected by many uncontrollable variables. It is important for every individual concerned about reimbursement policies for athletic training services to specifically address these issues with their individual legislators. Legislators need to be educated in relation to the importance of issues at hand and how they can help further the interest and efforts of their constituents. National legislation is affected by individual votes, and those votes can be influenced.

Strategic plans should be developed within each state to individually lobby national legislators regarding the creation and support for legislation relevant to the recognition of reimbursement for ath-

Table 6-2

JOINT COMMISSION ON SPORTS MEDICINE AND SCIENCE MEMBERS

American Academy of Family Physicians

American Academy of Pediatrics

American Academy of Pediatric Sports Medicine

American Association for Active Lifestyles and Fitness

American Association for Industrial Sports Medicine

American Chiropractic Association

American College Health Association

American College of Sports Medicine

American Dental Association

American Kinesiotherapy Association c/o American Academy of Physical Medicine and Rehabilitation

American Medical Association

American Medical Society for Sports Medicine

American Optometric Association Sports Vision Section

American Orthopedic Society for Sports Medicine

American Osteopathic Academy for Sports Medicine

American Osteopathic Association

American Physical Therapy Association Sports Physical Therapy Section

American Running and Fitness Association

American Society of Testing and Materials

Canadian Academy of Sports Medicine

Centers for Disease Control and Prevention

Coalition of Americans to Protect Sports

Joint Commissions on Sports Medicine and Science

National Association for Sports and Physical Education

National Association of Collegiate Directors of Athletics

National Association of Intercollegiate Athletics

National Collegiate Athletic Association

National Federation of State High School Associations

National Junior College Athletic Association

National Operating Committee on Standards for Athletic Equipment

National Strength and Conditioning Association

North American Society for Pediatric Exercise Medicine

Physiatric Association of Spine, Sports, and Occupational Rehabilitation

Sports Cardiovascular and Wellness Nutritionists

The President's Council on Physical Fitness and Sports

United States Consumer Products Safety Commission

United States Olympic Committee Sports Medicine Council

United States Olympic Committee Sports Medicine Society

letic training services. Every effort is needed at the local level to assist in affecting national policy. The significance and importance of these efforts cannot be overstated.

Often times athletic trainers have provider-client relationships with legislators or family members they have treated. These relationships clearly demonstrate the value of athletic training services and should be developed and maximized to benefit athletic trainers.

State Insurance Code Legislation

Landmark legislation was passed in the state of Georgia in 1999 that positively affected reimbursement for athletic trainers in that state. House Bill 93,[3] dealing with state insurance code, effective July 1, 1999, officially recognizes the athletic trainer as a health care provider in the state of Georgia (see Appendix 9). The bill states that if covered health care services are provided that are within the lawful scope of practice of an athletic trainer, then insurers must reimburse covered persons for such services. The bill does not mandate insurers to add any specific new covered benefits, nor does this law require any specific action by insurers to modify participating or preferred provider networks.

This legislation clearly and legally identifies the athletic trainer as a reimbursable entity and adds him or her to the list of other reimbursable health care providers. This legislation has and is being explored for adoption in other states.

OPPOSITION

It must be understood that efforts by athletic training competitors directed against establishing reimbursement for athletic training services are and will continue to be very aggressive. Competition for the very limited rehabilitation dollar is extremely intense and will continue to be so in the future. This must be clearly understood as every effort made on behalf of athletic trainers will generate equal or greater efforts against reimbursement recognition for athletic training services. It is beneficial to establish dialogue with these competing professions to attempt to identify common areas of concern and to promote collaborative efforts. Proceeding forward on a united front will achieve greater benefits for the rehabilitation professions and the patients who benefit from those services. However, previous history has indicated that these collaborative efforts are difficult to achieve.

CONCLUSION

Developing and employing creative strategies to achieve reimbursement for athletic training services is essential. The rapidly changing health care environment creates significant challenges in developing these strategies. The influence and effect of efforts from competitors further compounds the issues. A proactive, aggressive approach to developing these strategies is essential. All avenues must be pursued and all support must be garnered to realize the success in relation to these efforts. The previously discussed strategies provide a core of approaches that can be pursued. New strategies will be developed in the future.

REFERENCES

1. Focus on Therapeutic Outcomes. *Comparative Outcomes Analysis.* Knoxville, Tenn: Focus on Therapeutic Outcomes, Inc.; 1999.
2. Albohm, MJ, Wilkerson, GW. An outcomes assessment of care provided by certified athletic trainers. *Journal of Rehabilitation Outcomes Measurement.* 1999;3(3):51-56.

3. The State of Georgia House Bill 93, Georgia 145th General Assembly, 1999-2000 Regular Session, April 1999.

 *Chapter Seven*

The Future

OBJECTIVES

Following the completion of this chapter the reader will be able to:
- Identify future trends which may effect reimbursement for athletic trainers.
- Identify future trends for reimbursement in the traditional athletic training setting.
- Recognize the importance of Medicare recognition.
- Understand the role that reimbursement plays in the future development of the athletic training profession.

The unpredictable nature of current health care trends makes it difficult to predict the outcome of reimbursement efforts for athletic trainers. However, the time has never been better for athletic trainers to pursue this goal. Recent advances in achieving regulatory recognition and the wave of new health care providers entering the marketplace create opportunities never before available. Athletic training is in a perfect position to achieve reimbursable identity.

Clearly, change will continue to permeate and influence the health care marketplace. The shrinking dollar for rehabilitation services does not create a very optimistic picture for providers of services in this area. However, rehabilitation services are essential to patient outcomes, and providers who demonstrate effectiveness, efficiency, and value will be recognized and appropriately compensated.

The athletic trainer has historically operated in a managed care fashion, providing a continuum of care from prevention through rehabilitation. The skills of an athletic trainer go far beyond that of providing rehabilitative services to patients and clients. It is the role and model of the athletic trainer as a physician extender that should be emphasized when positioning the athletic trainer in the reimbursable health care marketplace. It is that professional profile that needs to be developed and highlighted, demonstrating a different or unique approach to providing traditional services rather than duplicating services in a model that already exists. Focusing on the traditional role and function of an athletic trainer should clearly illustrate that unique model. Athletic trainers are being reimbursed as physician extenders in clinical settings for a variety of services. These include evaluations and re-evaluations, exercise instruction, functional testing, activity modification, brace fitting, and other types of care. They are being reimbursed as physician extenders in outreach programs to secondary schools, health clubs, wellness centers, and industry by providing a variety of services, as well as serving as preventive exercise and movement modification specialists. The model is not that of a physical therapist assistant or aide but one demonstrating the full scope of skills that the athletic trainer possesses. It is this model that needs to be further developed and promoted in all settings, with all payers, throughout the country.

PREVENTION/WELLNESS

Reimbursement for prevention and wellness has not been a priority for the American health care system. Although evidence has existed for many years documenting the benefits of prevention and wellness activities on the health of our citizens, payers have been extremely reluctant to reimburse activities related to prevention and wellness. However, it is predicted that this will change in the future, primarily due to the influence of the baby boomer population, who has grown up realizing the disease prevention benefits of fitness and wellness.

If this change occurs, athletic trainers are in a perfect position to demonstrate their well-documented skills and expertise in the area of prevention, establishing their value as health care providers. For this to occur, however, it is imperative that the general public, payers, and other health care providers be thoroughly educated and informed regarding the unique skills of the athletic trainer in this area in order to fully recognize and utilize these valuable professionals.

Historically, the skills of the athletic trainer have sometimes been the best-kept secret. In today's health care arena and in the future, it will be the provider who demonstrates the greatest degree of effectiveness in the most efficient way, demonstrating the greatest value that will be the most recognized, utilized, and reimbursed. The skills of the athletic trainer must be aggressively marketed to those entities interested in purchasing these services in order for them to be fully integrated into the health care system of the future. It is projected that wellness and prevention activities will consume a significant portion of the health care dollar in the future and the athletic trainer is well positioned to take advantage of that emphasis, if he or she is recognized as the provider of choice for those services.

REIMBURSEMENT IN THE TRADITIONAL SETTING

An increasing number of college and university programs are beginning to pursue and implement reimbursement strategies for their athletic training programs. Revenue centers are being created in traditional athletic training room settings, and services once only available to intercollegiate athletes are now being made available to the campus community and general public.

Reimbursement for athletic training services at the secondary level may be slower to develop. The opportunities, similar to those at the collegiate setting, certainly exist, but a variety of logistical issues must be addressed. High schools typically do not have a billing system in place, nor do they have the ability to easily develop one. Numerous multiple payers exist due to variations in parental health insurance. Philosophical justification may be difficult to obtain; however, reimbursement models at the secondary level do exist and should be considered.

It is predicted that evidence of these reimbursement models in the traditional setting will increase throughout the country in the future and that the creation of for-profit entities within programs providing athletic training services will present extremely attractive business cases for the future. These particular models employ athletic trainers in their traditional setting and utilize their skills to the fullest degree in treating physically active people.

INDUSTRIAL SETTING

Athletic trainers in industrial settings continue to increase in number. Workers' compensation is an extremely large portion of the current health care market, consuming a significant portion of health care dollars. The health and welfare of the workforce is of extreme importance to government health care agencies, commercial payers, and managed care organizations. The athletic trainer is extremely qualified to provide a variety of health care services to this population through in-plant health care delivery systems. In models where athletic trainers are employed, outcomes demonstrate a significant financial savings in workers' compensation claims, a faster return to work rate, less time lost from work, and a higher degree of patient satisfaction with care provided. Athletic trainers also function as biomechanical analysts and ergonomic specialists in this setting and may also direct employee fitness/wellness programs.

FUTURE REIMBURSEMENT EFFORTS

Efforts to gain recognition for the athletic trainer as a reimbursable entity in the health care marketplace of today and tomorrow continue to be an extremely high priority for the National Athletic Trainers' Association (NATA). A new full-time director-level position in Governmental Relations and Reimbursement was added to the NATA national office staff in January 2001 to assist with these efforts.

Recent advances in reimbursement efforts have brought into focus clear goals for the future. Payer recognition is the number one priority. Regulatory codes are important and necessary to illustrate to payers that athletic training is recognized by the health care regulatory agencies, but those codes do not automatically ensure payment of claims.

Insurance companies must realize the role and benefit of athletic trainers. It is the payer who has the primary role in determining which services and providers are reimbursed. Recognition by the insurance industry requires state and national educational and public relations efforts directed at insurance companies and managed care organizations. A strong case must be presented, utilizing objective information such as outcomes data, to demonstrate the value of athletic training services. Data currently exist that clearly demonstrate the positive effect of athletic trainers on patient outcome and insurance claim reduction in the clinical as well as the traditional setting. It is logical to believe that insurance companies will value this demonstrated benefit if properly informed and educated. Demonstrating the value of athletic trainers in reducing insurance claims and other related health care costs is an extremely important designation to make, and this information must aggressively be delivered to the insurance industry.

Individual state athletic training associations must organize state reimbursement committees to plan and initiate specific approaches to targeted payers. The NATA Reimbursement Advisory Group (RAG) assists in state efforts and plans specific approaches to major payers on the national level. Influencing payer opinions at the state level is the key in achieving reimbursement.

HEALTH CARE FINANCING ADMINISTRATION RECOGNITION

Health Care Financing Administration (HCFA) recognition in the form of obtaining Medicare provider numbers for athletic trainers still remains the top priority for the future. Organized lobbying efforts on behalf of the athletic training profession are essential to achieving this goal. Although extremely costly, these efforts are essential to changing health care policy. Evidence of payer recognition at the state and national levels is extremely important and influential. Efforts on behalf of the NATA in the areas of governmental affairs and reimbursement, combined with these lobbying efforts, will create significant change in the future for reimbursement of athletic trainers.

CONCLUSION

The athletic trainer must become a reimbursable entity in order to assume the role of a valued and respected member of the health care provider community for today as well as the future. All efforts must be made, and initiatives pursued in order to make this become a reality. Reimbursement holds the key to the future of the profession of athletic training. If reimbursement is not achieved on a nationwide basis, employment opportunities for athletic trainers will be severely restricted and limited to the college/university and secondary school settings. Even in those settings, lack of reimbursement threatens position stability and employment for athletic trainers. Employers will choose professionals who are eligible for reimbursement over ones who are not if similar services are offered. Positioning the athletic trainer as a physician extender and utilizing his or her full range of skills will benefit reimbursement efforts. Collaborating with other health care professions seeking the same status will strengthen efforts. The future of the profession of athletic training cannot be ensured until widespread reimbursement is achieved.

Appendix 1

National Athletic Trainers' Association Approach to Payer Guidelines

Reprinted with permission from the National Athletic Trainers' Association.

I. Introduction

The following information is intended to give you, the certified athletic trainer, suggestions on how to pursue reimbursement for athletic training services in your state.

Because each state has different laws, rules and regulations governing athletic training, it is imperative that you understand your state laws in relation to reimbursement for athletic training services. It is also important that you understand your state laws governing the specific performance requirements for athletic training. A copy of your state practice act is enclosed in Section Six of this packet.

Remember that in states where you are regulated (licensed, registered, certified, or exempt), the law defines what you may do and not do. In states where you are not regulated, there are gray areas that may make some of the practice of athletic training subject to interpretation. In addition, you may be working under the extension of the license of another recognized health care provider (physicians, PTs, etc). States regulate health care providers in order to protect the public and "do no harm." Because of this, make sure you know your law before you undertake any of the following suggestions provided in this Approach to Payers Guidelines. We suggest that you obtain a legal interpretation of the statutes that regulate athletic training in your state. (Your state athletic training association may have this information).

Remember, reimbursement of athletic training is a group effort. We urge you to contact your state athletic training president, district director or Reimbursement Advisory Group representative prior to undertaking any attempts regarding reimbursement for athletic training services. We also encourage you to use the information contained in this packet.

II. Organization

    A. Organize a state reimbursement committee or add this task to the state governmental affairs committee or state corporate industrial clinical committee.

    B. Assign a reimbursement advisory group/committee chairperson to coordinate all reimbursement materials, issues and efforts. (We recommend that this person is the state president or a designee). Please inform the NATA Reimbursement Advisory Group chair as to who your state reimbursement contact is.

    C. Have your state reimbursement advisory group/committee develop an individual state packet for approaching payers. Add the materials that are enclosed in this packet.

    D. Tailor all of this material to meet your specific needs. Make sure you use specific information for your state, and include materials from team physicians, referring physicians, satisfied patients and important political leaders or legislators.

III. Legal Issues/Practice Act

    A. You must practice legally within the scope of your practice act or as a legal extender of the license of another health care provider in your state. (A copy of your state athletic training act is enclosed in Section Six of this packet).

    B. Have your state licensing board and/or other legal counsel obtain a ruling on whether athletic trainers can legally receive reimbursement for athletic training services. (Also check with governmental affairs for other state legal interpretations).

    C. If you cannot be legally reimbursed for your services under your present practice act, you may need to make changes in your practice act prior to approaching payers.

    D. If you do not have regulation, work with the governmental affairs committee in your state.

IV. Approaching the Payer (to be done only after Steps, I, II and III are complete).

    A. Develop a list of contacts:

        1. Identify individuals with in your state athletic training association. Individuals may work in the insurance field or have friends or relatives who are involved in insurance and can be of immense value in developing contacts.

        2. Identify individuals such as physicians, patients, politicians and legislators who may be influential in opening doors.

        3. Use your state insurance commissioner's office to obtain current lists of recognized insurance carriers/providers in your state. (See Insurance Company/Organization Information under Section Five for information on how to contact your state insurance commissioner). This may include small regional companies, large statewide carriers, as well as self-insured plans/ASO and indemnity groups. Your state insurance commissioner's office can provide the contacts, but it will be up to your state reimbursement advisory group/committee to evaluate the potential of each group or company based on your specific needs.

    B. Take the next step:

        1. Find out who the decision maker is in the insurance company. (Background information on several insurance companies is provided in this packet under Section Five). Obtain as much information about that person and the company as possible. For example, does the decision maker have a child who participates in high school athletics? If so, is there an ATC on staff at the high school who might be interested in assisting with your efforts? After completing your research, contact the decision maker in the insurance company and arrange an appointment. If an in-person meeting is not possible, send a letter to the decision maker requesting a clarification as to whether the company will reimburse for services. A sample letter can be found in Section Five.

        2. If you are meeting in person, try to host the meeting at your clinic and provide a tour of your facility. Make sure the clinic administrator and VFO are informed and supportive of your efforts, and are aware of the meeting. Have select physicians meet with payer representatives to share positive testimony of ATCs. Physicians are key here and should be used as a resource.

        3. Be prepared, provide answers, be able to discuss specific costs and prices, be able to explain why athletic training services should be included. Use the NATA Outcomes Study statistics as published in the enclosed article Titled "An Outcomes Assessment of Care Provided by Certified Athletic Trainers." (See Section Eight). Remember to focus on athletic training services as managed care products, not just fee-for-service contracts. A visit satisfaction survey from your particular clinic, focusing on patient contact with ATCs, could be helpful!

        Have copies of the information contained in this packet available for your guest. For example, the letter regarding the Uniform Billing Code (Section Four) could be a valuable part of your presentation. In addition, provide copies of information on your state athletic training organization.

A sample Power Point presentation is included in Section Eight of this packet. Feel free to use as much of this presentation as you wish. If you would like this presentation sent to you via e-mail or computer disk, contact Richard Rogers at richr@nata.org or (800) 879-6282, ext. 103. Samples of other promotional items are also included in Section Eight. Brochures for your presentation are provided in the side pocket of this booklet. If you need additional copies, contact Richard Rogers.

4. A list of frequently asked questions and answers is also included in Section Eight. Look at these questions carefully, and make sure you understand the information presented.

5. If you feel uncomfortable with presenting this information, please contact one of the representatives to the Reimbursement Advisory Group for tips. (See Section Nine for a roster of all committee members). We are here to help you!

6. Remember that the NATA is a professional organization, so act professionally at all times. Analyze the advantages/disadvantages of a specific contract. Do not sell your profession short.

7. Share all information with the NATA Reimbursement Advisory Group. A reimbursement response/update form is enclosed in Section Nine of this packet for your convenience.

V. Successes/Failures

    A. Regardless of the outcome of the meeting, send a thank-you note to the payer representative! This may seem like a small detail, but it is very important!

    B. Sometimes, in order to succeed you must fail. A number of successes have come out of an initial denial from an insurance provider. Each failure may help redesign your approach to successful reimbursement. Be patient and do not give up!

    C. If a claim is denied, contact the company and ask why the claim was denied. Challenges to denials are common and expected and often result in payment. Set up a meeting to obtain as much information as you can on why the denial was made, if denial continues. Lobbying by patients is sometimes effective in influencing payers.

    D. Focus on educating the company on the specific athletic training services you provide.

VI. Communication/Support—NATA RAG

    A. Reimbursement is not an individual effort. Coordinate your efforts with those individuals at the national level, including the NATA Reimbursement Advisory chair.

    B. Request support from the NATA Reimbursement Advisory Group.

        1. Legal interpretations

        2. Fact finding

        3. Crafting strategic approaches

    C. NATA Reimbursement Advisory Group members are available to accompany state representatives to meetings with payers. A roster of representatives is enclosed under Section Nine.

VII. Industrial Athletic Training:

    A. Contact individuals in other states who have experience in industrial athletic training.

        1. Become familiar with the various reimbursement models common to this setting.

    B. Who to contact in industry:

        1. Human resources director

        2. Safety or risk manager

        3. Senior management CEO, CFO or COO

        4. Plant medical director

    C. What facts involving health care expenditures can help you open the door?

        1. One trillion dollars spent annually on health care!

2. Fourteen percent of the United States gross national product is spent on health care.

3. General Motors spends more on health care than on its steel!

4. Seventy percent of industrial illness is preventable, especially repetitive trauma.

D. What can we as athletic trainers provide?

1. Injury prevention programs

2. Ergonomics/job site analysis

3. Case management

4. Rehabilitation, especially involving acute trauma and repetitive injury

5. Fitness/wellness education programs

E. Benefits of program

1. Reduced workers compensation & group medical costs

2. Reduced light duty days

3. Improved productivity & employee morale

4. Improved employee attraction and retention

5. Quality control

6. Improved ergonomics

7. Case management

8. Injury prevention

 *Appendix 2*

Medicare, CPT Codes, and UB Code Rulings

Reprinted with permission from the National Athletic Trainers' Association.

T. Lane Macalester
202.663.8894
lane.macalester@shawpittman.com
November 1, 1999

By Scheduled Express

Eve Becker-Doyle, CAE
Executive Director
National Athletic Trainers' Association
2952 Stemmons Freeway
Dallas, TX 75247

Re: Medicare Regulatory Issues Governing Certified Athletic Trainers

Dear Ms. Becker-Doyle:

You have requested that we review briefly the issue of whether Medicare laws prohibit certified athletic trainer (ATCs) from providing outpatient rehabilitation services to commercial patients in clinics in which Medicare patients also are treated and, further, whether Medicare prohibits reimbursement for services provided by ATCs.

We are not aware of any Medicare prohibition against ATC's providing outpatient rehabilitation services to commercial patients in Medicare-certified outpatient rehabilitation clinics or comprehensive outpatient rehabilitation facilities (CORFs). This was confirmed to us by representatives at the Health Care Financing Administration (HCFA), the agency that administers the Medicare program.

Further, while the applicable Medicare statutes and regulations do not expressly prohibit ATCs from providing outpatient physical therapy services to Medicare patients under certain conditions, HCFA indicated that it currently does not authorize Medicare reimbursement for outpatient physical therapy services rendered by a provider other than a licensed physical therapist or a licensed physical therapy assistant under the supervision of a licensed physical therapist.

We are continuing to research these issues in more depth as NATA determines strategies for proceeding.

Sincerely,

T. Lane Macalester

cc: Sarah A.B. Teslik, Esq.

Appendix 3

Fact Sheet on Athletic Training and the National Athletic Trainers' Association

Reprinted with permission from the NATA.

PROFESSIONAL PROFILE

Certified athletic trainers work under the supervision of a licensed physician and specialize in the recognition, treatment, and rehabilitation of injuries incurred by athletes and those engaged in physical activity. Athletic training is recognized as an allied health care profession by the American Medical Association (AMA), and education programs are accredited by the AMA's Commission on Accreditation of Allied Health Educational Programs.

Certification standards are established by the National Athletic Trainers' Association Board of Certification (NATABOC). In order to obtain certification as an athletic trainer, an individual must possess a bachelor's degree from an accredited college or university; complete athletic training experience hours under the supervision of a NATABOC certified athletic trainer; and pass a written practical and written simulation examination administered by the NATABOC. After an athletic trainer is certified, he or she must obtain 80 hours of continuing education units within a 3-year reporting term to maintain certification.

The NATABOC is a member of the National Organization of Competency Assurance in Washington, D.C. Annually, the Board of Certification reviews the requirements for certification eligibility and continuing education standards. Additionally the Board reviews and revises the certification examination in accordance to the test specifications of a Role Delineation Study that was validated in 1999.

At the time of this writing, 36 states regulate athletic training. (A complete list of states and the type of regulation is located in Section Six.) In addition, the following states are seeking regulation: Arizona, Michigan, Nevada, Utah, Washington and Maryland.

Georgia recently passed legislation providing for reimbursement under insurance policies for services within the scope of practice of athletic trainers. While this action is unusual, we feel the state of Georgia has set a precedent and we are confident that other states will soon follow this path. A copy of the Georgia legislation is also enclosed in Section Six.

It is documented that certified athletic trainers provide a high level of patient satisfaction. In a national outcomes study of athletic training services, published in the Journal of Rehabilitation Outcomes Measurement and a copy of which is provided in Section Eight, it is proven that "certified athletic trainers effect a change in the function and quality of life outcomes of individuals with musculoskeletal disorders."

ASSOCIATION PROFILE

The National Athletic Trainers' Association (NATA) is a not-for-profit organization with more than 26,000 members worldwide. The NATA is committed to advancing, encouraging and improving the athletic training profession.

Founded in 1950 with a membership of 200 athletic trainers, the NATA is based in Dallas, Texas, and provides a variety of services to its membership, including continuing education, governmental affairs and public relations. The NATA also publishes the Journal of Athletic Training, a quarterly scientific journal, and the NATA News, a monthly membership magazine.

The mission of the National Athletic Trainers' Association is to enhance the quality of healthcare for athletes and those engaged in physical activity, and to advance the profession of athletic training through education and research in the prevention, evaluation, management and rehabilitation of injuries.

Appendix 4

An Outcomes Assessment of Care Provided by Certified Athletic Trainers

Reprinted with permission from Albohm MJ, Wilkerson GB. An outcomes assessment of care provided by certified athletic trainers. *J Rehabil Outcomes Meas*. 1999;3(3):51-56.

Outcomes assessment is an important determination in evaluating health-related quality of life. Changes in health-related quality of life are important concerns for patients, providers, and payers. The purpose of this investigation was to assess the effect of care provided by National Athletic Trainers' Association Board Of Certification (NATABOC) Certified Athletic Trainers on health-related quality of life outcomes in various practice settings. A non-randomized prospective functional status and quality-of-life outcomes assessment was conducted on 4,939 individuals, with physician diagnosed musculoskeletal injury, treated by NATABOC Certified Athletic Trainers at 125 sites throughout the United States. Results indicated significant change in all outcomes variables measured, with the greatest change in functional outcomes and physical outcomes. This investigation indicates that care provided by NATABOC Certified Athletic Trainers effects a change in health-related quality of life patient outcomes.

Key words: certified athletic trainers, functional outcomes, musculoskeletal injury

INTRODUCTION

In recent years, there has been much discussion of the need for health care providers to measure "outcomes" as a means of demonstrating quality of care.[1] Terms like outcomes management, outcomes assessment, outcomes-based practice, functional outcomes, outcomes evaluation, and clinical outcome measures are commonly used to describe relationships among healthcare practice and patient function.[2] The term "Outcome" remains poorly defined, and procedures for measuring outcomes lack standardization. A positive medical outcome is generally associated with restoration of function. However, the term "function" can have variable meanings, and determination of "optimal function" is dependent on expectations relative to an individual's performance capabilities.[2,3]

Health-related quality of life (HRQL) is a multidimensional construct that includes an individual's physical, functional, emotional, and social well-being relative to his or her actual and anticipated levels of functioning.[4,5] The underlying assumption of outcomes assessment is that specific treatment processes contribute to improvement in numerous interrelated performance capabilities that contribute to overall human function, thereby enhancing HRQL.

Patients are an excellent source of information about their own conditions and treatments. A patient's experiences and opinions about what worked are important because it is ultimately the patient's responsibility to perpetuate the positive effects produced by medical care. Hence, routine and standardized collection of patient-centered information is essential to assess and ultimately improve the effectiveness of injury care.[2,3]

For many years, the certified athletic trainer (ATC) has served in a key role as the coordinator of health care for athletes in high school, college, and professional sport athletic programs. Working close-ly with team physicians, the ATC provides specialized services related to injury prevention, therapeu-tic care, and rehabilitation. In recent years, increasing demand for such services from the physically active population has dramatically increased the number of ATCs working in non-athletic settings, such as sports medicine clinics, physician offices, and worksite industrial clinics.

The primary purpose of this investigation was to assess the effect of care provided by certified ath-letic trainers on HRQL outcomes among patients treated in sports medicine clinics, high school ath-letic training rooms college/university athletic training rooms, and industrial worksite clinics.

MATERIALS/METHODS

The principal methodology of traditional medical research has been controlled experimentation, consisting of prospective, randomized clinical trials, and quantification of variables that can be meas-ured with a high degree of precision. Outcome indicators are not absolute measures, such as tempera-ture or weight; they are related to social norms and expectations.[6] Transition in focus from the effect of a specific intervention on an isolated physiologic function to the varied possible effects of medical care on patient function within society requires different methodology. Experimental research designs are rarely possible in social science research, which seeks to measure complex behaviors and feelings related to concepts, such as well being and quality of life.[5]

There has been increasing acceptance of global health status measures of HRQL, such as the SF-36.[7-12] Early versions of general health status and quality of life outcomes measures were designed for evaluating chronic illness and disability in sedentary populations. Attention has been directed at meas-uring outcomes in a more active population.

A specific instrument designed to measure improvements in function among physically active sub-jects whose preinjury functional capabilities and post-treatment expectations exceed that of the gener-al population was developed[13] (Figure A4-1). The instrument was validated, over three consecutive 6 month clinical trial periods, by correlating the qualitative individual and grouped item outcomes results, as rated by patients and providers, with the pre- and post-treatment quantitative assessments made by independent therapists. The instrument was revised after each period until correlations for each outcomes variable reached established predefined values.

The instrument assesses individual and group factors including functional outcomes (activities of daily living function, work activities, sport/recreation/wellness activities), physical outcomes (move-ment capacity, strength/power capacity, endurance capacity, motor abilities, body structure impair-ment, sensory), general health status, specific medical condition, and psychosocial status. The overall outcome is a compilation of all individual factors. In addition, at discharge, a patient satisfaction rat-ing is obtained (Figure Appendix 4-1).

A nonrandomized perspective functional status and quality of life assessment was conducted utiliz-ing the previously described instrument from February 1, 1996 through August 1, 1998 on 4,939 patients with physician diagnosed musculoskeletal injury. Patients were selected in a consecutive man-ner. These patients were treated by National Athletic Trainers' Association Board of Certification (NATABOC)[14] certified Athletic Trainers. Specific treatment prescriptions were provided by referring physicians. Patient pre- and post-treatment status was assessed.

Definition of terms, an explanation of rating scales and specific instrument administration proce-dures are specifically outlined in a detailed user's guide.[15] The instrument was self-administered during

Patient—Your responses to this questionnaire will help your athletic trainer and this clinic determine rehabilitation outcomes for specific medical conditions in response to specific treatments. This will help us optimize our treatment services to you and other patients. Your responses will be kept confidential, and will not affect your care in any way. Thanks for your assistance.

AT INTAKE

AT DISCHARGE

Instructions: Please rate your current capacities specific to the injury for which you will receive, or have received, treatments. Please answer all questions as best you can, even if some of the questions seem somewhat irrelevant to you. Circle the appropriate response according to the (0 1 2 3 4) scale; 0 = critical problem, 1 = severe problem, 2 = moderate problem, 3 = minor problem, 4 = no problem.

AT INTAKE		AT DISCHARGE
0 1 2 3 4	**General health**—feel good, happy, energetic, active, relaxed, free of medication, free of pain/discomfort, appetite, nutrition, body composition (body weight; obesity, anorexia) . . .	0 1 2 3 4
0 1 2 3 4	**Specific medical condition**—status of injury, illness, surgery . . .	0 1 2 3 4
0 1 2 3 4	**Daily living activities**—sleeping, sitting, standing, walking, climbing stairs, dressing, personal care, studying (reading, writing, typing/computer), traveling, driving, personal business affairs . . .	0 1 2 3 4
0 1 2 3 4	**Work activities**—lifting/lowering, holding/handling, carrying, pushing/pulling, bending over, squatting/stooping, kneeling, crawling, reaching, turning/pivoting, gripping/pinching, fingering . . .	0 1 2 3 4
0 1 2 3 4	**Sports/recreation/wellness activities**—running, jumping, throwing, catching, kicking, swinging, withstanding impacts, weightlifting, specific sport/recreation/wellness activity . . .	0 1 2 3 4
0 1 2 3 4	**Movement**—getting into desired positions, range of motion, speed of motion, bilateral differences, (e.g., limping), need for support device . . .	0 1 2 3 4
0 1 2 3 4	**Strength/power**—applying adequate force, applying force at necessary speeds or frequencies	0 1 2 3 4
0 1 2 3 4	**Endurance**—sustaining a movement pattern over a long period of time, sustaining a faster paced or more strenuous movement pattern over a short period of time	0 1 2 3 4
0 1 2 3 4	**Motor abilities**—motor control, coordination, balance, agility, reflexes . . .	0 1 2 3 4
0 1 2 3 4	**Body structure**—swelling, inflammation, atrophy, deformity, posture, bilateral differences, joint stability, muscle spasms . . .	0 1 2 3 4
0 1 2 3 4	**Sensory**—pain, sensitivity, discomfort, numbness . . .	0 1 2 3 4
0 1 2 3 4	**Psycho-social status**—confidence, anxiety, self-esteem, hopeful, depression, socialization, dependence, isolation . . .	0 1 2 3 4

At discharge, please rate your satisfaction with the treatment services provided, and your athletic trainer. Optional—circle any aspects that you were not satisfied with. List other concerns.

Satisfaction with treatment services: Treatment Schedule—scheduling, following schedule, accessibility; Facility—location, parking, appearance, equipment; Treatment Environment—physical, social; Billing, if relevant—explanation, procedures   0 1 2 3 4

Satisfaction with your athletic trainer: Communications, professionalism; Therapy—appropriate to my needs, effective   0 1 2 3 4

(AT INTAKE scale: –CRITICAL PROBLEM, –SEVERE PROBLEM, –MODERATE PROBLEM, –MINOR PROBLEM, –NO PROBLEM)

(AT DISCHARGE scale: –CRITICAL PROBLEM, –SEVERE PROBLEM, –MODERATE PROBLEM, –MINOR PROBLEM, –NO PROBLEM)

(Satisfaction scale: very unsatisfied, unsatisfied, moderately satisfied, satisfied, very satisfied)

Figure A4-1. To be completed by patient at intake and discharge.

the patient's initial evaluation and the provider assessment was completed following patient evaluation and prior to the initiation of treatment. Both patient and provider completed the post-treatment assessment at discharge, following the termination of treatment. Completed forms were sent to a central repository for data entry.

There has been increasing acceptance of global health status measures of health-related quality of life.

Patient—Your responses to this questionnaire will help your athletic trainer and this clinic determine rehabilitation outcomes for specific medical conditions in response to specific treatments. This will help us optimize our treatment services to you and other patients. Your responses will be kept confidential, and will not affect your care in any way. Thanks for your assistance.

Patient Demographics

Study subject average age was 27.31 years and 60 percent of the subjects were male. Previous injury episodes and comorbid conditions were recorded for each subject, as well as injury location, injury diagnosis, severity of injury, type of treatment provided, treatment number/duration in days, number of treatments/frequency of treatments, and number of days between injury and initiation of treatment. In addition, information was obtained related to patient referral source and payer.

Statistical Analysis

Data were accessed from a central study database and statistically analyzed. Pre- and post-treatment evaluation questions were rated on a zero to four scale (0 = critical problem, 1 = severe problem, 2 = moderate problem, 3 = minor problem, 4 = no problem). Values expressed were the average of the ratings and the percent of change.

The standard response mean (SRM) was utilized to measure the difference between the pre and post-treatment ratings (SRM = meanpost — meanpre/SdPost-Pre).[12,16] Statistically, the SRM is similar to the paired t-value or ANOVA for the difference between pre- and post-test scores, in that the coefficient represents the ratio of the variance between groups to the variance within groups. The SRM has been shown to be a valid method of comparing patient improvements between two or more variables or populations with unequal Ns.[12,16] Statistical significance is obtained by converting the SRM to a "t" by multiplying the SRM by the square root of the N.

Results

The patients' and athletic trainers' assessments of pre- and post-treatment status were relatively consistent, with the athletic trainers' assessments of port-treatment improvements being somewhat higher than the patients'.

The Greatest changes occurred in Functional Outcomes (pre = 2.16, post = 3.48, SRM = 1.49), specifically in work activities and sport/recreation activities, and in Physical Outcomes (pre = 2.35, post = 3.56, SRM = 1.49). Treatment intervention was less relevant in affecting general health and psychosocial status. A high degree of patient satisfaction (3.89) was expressed with treatment provided by athletic trainers (Table A4-1).

Changes in outcomes were significant (p<0.0001) across all site types and payer groups (see Tables A4-2 and A4-3).

DISCUSSION

Patients in this study were not randomized to treatments or individual providers. Therefore, individual approaches to specific treatments may vary. The date also does not account for subtle changes

Table A4-1

TOTAL OUTCOMES (ACROSS ALL INJURY LOCATIONS, DIAGNOSES, AND TREATMENTS; RATINGS ON 0 TO 4 SCALE; N = 4,939)(SIGNIFICANCE $P < 0.0001$)

Outcomes Variable	Patient Assessment				Athletic Trainer Assessment			
	Pre-	Post-	% Inc	SRM	Pre-	Post-	% Inc	SRM
Overall Outcomes	2.41	3.56	48	1.60	2.42	3.64	51	1.91
Functional Outcomes:	2.16	3.48	61	1.49	2.14	3.56	67	1.80
activities of daily living	2.57	3.68	43	1.10	2.51	3.75	49	1.41
work activities	2.16	3.47	61	1.25	2.16	3.58	65	1.51
sport/recreation activities	1.75	3.30	89	1.41	1.73	3.36	94	1.71
Physical Outcomes:	2.35	3.56	51	1.49	2.34	3.65	56	1.81
movement	2.18	3.56	63	1.32	2.24	3.68	64	1.54
strength	2.19	3.49	60	1.25	2.13	3.55	66	1.55
endurance	2.31	3.51	52	1.13	2.17	3.54	63	1.47
motor abilities	2.87	3.73	30	0.86	2.72	3.78	39	1.15
body structure	2.46	3.61	47	1.12	2.50	3.72	49	1.36
sensory	2.10	3.47	65	1.34	2.27	3.61	59	1.48
general health status	2.79	3.63	31	0.89	3.12	3.78	21	0.82
specific medical condition	2.14	3.48	62	1.43	2.15	3.54	65	1.72
psycho-social status	3.36	3.83	14	0.56	3.32	3.85	16	0.69
patient satisfaction—treatments		3.87						
patient satisfaction—athletic trainer		3.89						

Table A4-2

OUTCOMES, BY SITE TYPE (ACROSS ALL INJURY LOCATIONS, DIAGNOSES, AND TREATMENTS) (SIGNIFICANCE P < 0.0001)

	All Site Types	Sports Med Clinics	High School Training Room	College/ University Training Room	Industrial Setting
Variable	N = 4939	N = 2145	N = 868	N = 906	N = 802
Overall outcomes	pre- 2.41	pre- 2.24	pre - 2.50	pre- 2.62	pre- 2.44
	post- 3.56	post- 3.39	post- 3.75	post- 3.71	post- 3.60
	SRM 1.60	SRM 1.58	SRM 1.74	SRM 1.54	SRM 1.58
Functional outcomes	pre- 2.16	pre- 1.96	pre- 2.29	pre- 2.4	pre- 2.17
	post- 3.48	post- 3.26	post-3.71	post- 3.69	post- 3.53
	SRM 1.49	SRM 1.47	SRM 1.56	SRM 1.42	SRM 1.53
Physical outcomes	pre- 2.35	pre- 2.19	pre- 2.39	pre- 2.58	pre- 2.43
	post- 3.56	post- 3.39	post- 3.73	post-3.71	post- 3.62
	SRM 1.49	SRM 1.49	SRM 1.62	SRM 1.42	SRM 1.42
ADL function	pre- 2.57	pre- 2.41	pre- 2.68	pre- 2.82	pre- 2.50
	post-3.68	post- 3.52	post- 3.83	post- 3.83	post- 3.68
	SRM 1.10	SRM 1.09	SRM 1.13	SRM 1.04	SRM 1.18
Work activities function	pre- 2.16	pre- 1.905	pre- 2.37	pre- 2.48	pre- 2.04
	post- 3.47	post- 3.27	post- 3.71	post- 3.67	post- 3.49
	SRM 1.25	SRM 1.23	SRM 1.29	SRM 1.17	SRM 1.38
Sports/recreation wellness function	pre- 1.75	pre- 1.51	pre- 1.83	pre- 2.03	pre- 1.97
	post- 3.30	post- 2.99	post- 3.57	post- 3.58	post- 3.43
	SRM 1.41	SRM 1.39	SRM 1.55	SRM 1.43	SRM 1.29

in patients' conditions over time and the treatment adjustments that occur in response to these changes. Data generated were collected by a variety of providers at multiple locations. Variables associated with these factors need to be reduced in future studies to facilitate interpretation of predictive models. Standardized data collection procedures were implemented to address these issues and to minimize the effect of these variables. The large sample size (4,939) certainly contributes to the significance of difference demonstrated.

This investigation provides information not previously reported concerning the relationship between treatment and health related outcomes. Although outcomes studies cannot provide the same rigorous controls as randomized clinical trials, they can provide valuable information for conceptualizing efficient and effective future trials.

This study contributes to the body of knowledge related to health care outcomes resulting from therapeutic interventions provided by certified athletic trainers in the management of musculoskeletal disorders in a physically active population.

Table A4-3

OUTCOMES BY PAYER (ACROSS ALL INJURY LOCATIONS, DIAGNOSES, AND TREATMENTS) (SIGNIFICANCE $P < 0.0001$)

Variable	All Payers	Medicaid	Medicare	Mgd. Care	Work Comp	Champus	Private Ins.	Insti. Ins.	Patient
	N = 4964	N = 38	N = 118	N = 399	N = 644	N = 31	N = 1552	N = 1977	N = 205
Overall	Pre 2.41	Pre 2.00	Pre 2.23	Pre 2.31	Pre 2.14	Pre 2.48	Pre 2.36	Pre 2.56	Pre 2.45
Outcomes	Post 3.56	Post 3.21	Post 3.13	Post 3.40	Post 3.37	Post 3.34	Post 3.54	Post 3.70	Post 3.68
	SRM 1.60	SRM 1.44	SRM 1.47	SRM 1.48	SRM 1.53	SRM 1.38	SRM 1.67	SRM 1.65	SRM 1.50
Functional	Pre 2.16	Pre 1.79	Pre 1.94	Pre 2.04	Pre 1.82	Pre 2.17	Pre 2.10	Pre 2.34	Pre 2.26
Outcomes	Post 3.48	Post 3.04	Post 2.94	Post 3.27	Post 3.24	Post 3.19	Post 3.45	Post 3.66	Post 3.65
	SRM 1.49	SRM 1.30	SRM 1.28	SRM 1.39	SRM 1.47	SRM 1.34	SRM 1.54	SRM 1.53	SRM 1.38
Physical	Pre 2.35	Pre 2.02	Pre 2.20	Pre 2.25	Pre 2.11	Pre 2.52	Pre 2.31	Pre 2.49	Pre 2.35
Outcomes	Post 3.56	Post 3.22	Post 3.14	Post 3.41	Post 3.38	Post 3.37	Post 3.53	Post 3.70	Post 3.66
	SRM 1.49	SRM 1.35	SRM 1.33	SRM 1.40	SRM 1.42	SRM 1.24	SRM 1.56	SRM 1.51	SRM 1.47
ADL	Pre 2.57	Pre 2.08	Pre 2.39	Pre 2.57	Pre 2.26	Pre 2.65	Pre 2.51	Pre 2.71	Pre 2.69
Function	Post 3.68	Post 3.26	Post 3.23	Post 3.54	Post 3.48	Post 3.39	Post 3.66	Post 3.81	Post 3.77
	SRM 1.10	SRM 1.16	SRM 0.97	SRM 0.93	SRM 1.13	SRM 0.93	SRM 1.17	SRM 1.11	SRM 0.96
Work	Pre 2.16	Pre 1.79	Pre 1.81	Pre 2.03	Pre 1.54	Pre 2.32	Pre 2.16	Pre 2.40	Pre 2.31

Table A4-3 continued

	All Payers	Medicaid	Medicare	Mgd. Care	Work Comp	Champus	Private Ins.	Insti. Ins.	Patient
Sports/Rec	Pre 1.75	Pre 1.50	Pre 1.63	Pre 1.51	Pre 1.67	Pre 1.55	Pre 1.64	Pre 1.91	Pre 1.78
Wellness	Post 3.30	Post 2.79	Post 2.62	Post 2.98	Post 3.12	Post 2.97	Post 3.22	Post 3.51	Post 3.51
Function	SRM 1.41	SRM 1.01	SRM 1.02	SRM 1.36	SRM 1.24	SRM 1.29	SRM 1.46	SRM 1.47	SRM 1.53
Function	SRM 1.25	SRM 1.29	SRM 1.09	SRM 1.19	SRM 1.44	SRM 1.06	SRM 1.23	SRM 1.24	SRM 1.2
Activities	Post 3.47	Post 3.08	Post 2.96	Post 3.29	Post 3.12	Post 3.23	Post 3.46	Post 3.66	Post 3.66

CONCLUSION

The results of this study indicate that treatment provided by NATABOC certified athletic trainers effect a change in the function and quality of life outcomes of individuals with musculoskeletal disorders.

REFERENCES

1. A. Donabedian. "The Quality of care: How Can It Be Assessed." *Journal of the American Medical Association* 260 (1988): 1743-1748

2. S.C. Robertson and A.S. Colborn. "Outcomes Research for Rehabilitation: Issues and Solutions." *Journal of Rehabilitation Outcomes Measurements* 1, no. 5 (1997): 15-23.

3. C.W. Pa and T.T.H. Wan. "Confirmatory Analysis of Health Outcome Indicators: The 36-Item Short-Form Health Survey (SF-36)" *Journal of Rehabilitation Outcomes Measurement* 1, no.2 (1997): 438-59.

4. G.J. Wan et al. "A Framework for Organizing Health-Related Quality of Life Research." *Journal of Rehabilitation Outcomes Measurement* 1, no. 2 (1997): 31-37.

5. L.B. Wilson and P.D. Cleary. "Linking Clinical Variables with Health-Related Quality of Life: A Conceptual Model of Patient Outcomes." *Journal of the American Medical Association* 273 (1995): 59-65.

6. R.A. Keith. "Conceptual Basis of Outcome Measures." *American Journal of Physical Medicine and Rehabilitation* 74 (1995): 73-80.

7. R.H. Brook and C.J. Kamberg. "General Health Status Measures and Outcome Measurement: A Commentary on Measuring Functional Status." *Journal of Chronic Diseases* 40 (1987): 1315.

8. Health Outcomes Institute: An introduction to the Health Institute's outcomes management system: intro to the OMS. March, 1993.

9. Health Outcomes Institute: Outcomes measurement instrumentation: intro to the OMS. April, 1993.

10. C.A. McHorney et al. "The MOS 36 Item Short Form Health Survey (SF-36): III. Test of Data Quality, Scaling Assumptions, and Reliability Across Diverse Patient Groups." *Medical Care* 32 (1994): 40-66.

11. C.A. McHorney et al. "The MOS 36 Item Short Form Health Survey (SF-36): II. Psychometric and Clinical Test of Validity in Measuring Physical and Mental Health Constructs." *Medical Care* 31 (1993): 247-263.

12. M.H. Liang MH et al. Comparison of Five Health Status Instruments for Orthopaedic Evaluation. *Medical Care* 28 (1990): 632-642.

13. BIO*Analysis Systems. 408-B Bayview Dr., PO Box 4805, Frisco, CO 80443-4805.

14. National Athletic Trainers' Association Board of Certification, Inc., 1512 South 60th St., Omaha, NE. 68106-2102.

15. *Athletic Training Outcomes Assessment Users Guide.* (Frisco, CO: BIO*Analysis Systems,1996).

16. P.W. Stratford et al. "Health Status Measures: Strategies and Analytic Methods for Assessing Change Scores." *Physical Therapy* 76, no. 10 (1996): 109-1123.

Appendix 5

Request for Proposals—Athletic Training Outcomes Assessment Data

Reprinted with permission from the National Athletic Trainers' Association

INTRODUCTION

The NATA Research and Education Foundation, through its Research Committee, is acting as gate-keeper for the database from the nationwide 1996-1998 Athletic Training Outcomes Assessment. Preliminary reports from the Outcomes Assessment have been published at regular intervals in the monthly newsletter of the National Athletic Trainers' Association, NATA News. Now available for further analysis is the raw data from more than 6,000 patients who received 90% or more of their care from certified athletic trainers. These outcomes data were collected at numerous venues throughout the United States, including sports medicine clinics, high schools, colleges, universities, and industrial settings. Access to the 1996-1998 Athletic Training Outcomes Assessment database will be limited to principal investigators who have submitted research proposals approved and funded by the NATA Research and Education Foundation.

BACKGROUND

Historically, physicians, particularly orthopedic surgeons, have used injury-specific, objective evaluation systems to assess the results of their treatment and to evaluate patient function, e.g., International Knee Documentation Committee (IKDC) evaluation form, the American Shoulder and Elbow Surgeons' Shoulder evaluation form. In the last decade, generic measures of the patient's assessment of his or her behavioral functioning, subjective sense of well-being, and perception of health have been developed and used to assess the health status of patients with general and chronic diseases, e.g., SF-36. These evaluative tools inquire about the patient's vitality, their level of general and mental health and levels of physical and social functioning following illness or injury. The responsibility for treatment and rehabilitation of musculoskeletal injuries among the physically active is shared by a growing number of allied health practitioners. Certified athletic trainers are well positioned in clinics and hospitals, secondary schools, colleges and universities, and industrial settings to provide needed physical medicine services to these patients. Outcomes of treatment in athletic training and sports medicine include but are not limited to: (a) patient assessment of a particular treatment intended to eliminate his/her specific physical impairment, (b) patient-reported evaluation of function and functional limitations experienced during activities of daily living, work, sport and/or recreational activity; and (c) patient assessment of his/her ability to perform sport, recreational or work at pre-injury activity levels. Studies are needed to evaluate the utilization of health care resources, e.g., the number of visits the patient made to the certified athletic trainer, the equipment and/or supplies issued to the patient in the course of treatment. Of similar importance is the level of satisfaction the patient has with the caregiver and/or the support staff, and with the overall results of treatment. Outcomes research is needed in athletic training and sports medicine to determine the effectiveness of a particular intervention, treatment methodology, or rehabilitation protocol for sports-related injuries. Moreover, outcomes research is needed to validate the quality of care provided by certified athletic trainers in comparison with reported patients' evaluations of their outcomes for treatment provided by physiatrists; board-certified physical therapists, specifically specialists compared with non-specialists; physical therapist assistants; and/or non-licensed clinical staff members.

OBJECTIVES

The Research and Education Foundation requests top-caliber research proposals that: 1) seek to determine the effectiveness of athletic trainer interventions, treatment methodologies, or rehabilitation protocols for sports-related injuries, and 2) to validate the quality of care provided by certified athletic trainers. Will use the database from the nationwide 1996-1998 NATA-Athletic Training Outcomes Assessment. To this end, the Research and Education Foundation offers access to the database from the nationwide 1996-1998 Athletic Training Outcomes Assessment Research Report. The Foundation seeks proposals that can effectively utilize the database to initiate new studies or support existing research in outcomes assessment.

CONTENT OF THE DATABASE

The NATA Athletic Training Outcomes Assessment Research Report includes data in the following categories:
- Across all injury locations, injury types, and treatments.
- Within each site type classification (N > 10)
- Within each referring source classification (N > 10)
- Within each payer classification (N > 10)
- Within each injury location (n > 10)
- Within each injury type (n > 10)
- Within each treatment (n > 10)

In each category are:
- "Outcomes"
- Special Analyses (for "Across all injury locations, injury types, & treatments" only)
- Each analysis describes the athletic trainers in the ATOA database; and the respective site type, referring source, payer, injury location, injury type, and treatment.

The "Outcomes" include the average "Pre-" and "Post-" treatment ratings (on the 0-4 scale) for each population, the percentage increase from Pre- to the Post- ratings, and the SRM (Standardized Response Mean) value, according to the PATIENT and ATHLETIC TRAINER assessments, for each outcomes assessment variable. The outcomes assessment variables include:

1. OVERALL OUTCOMES—a composite of #4-15
2. Functional Outcomes—a composite of #6-8
3. Physical Outcomes—a composite of #9-14
4. general health status
5. specific medical condition
6. activities of daily living function

7. work activities of daily living function
8. sport/recreation/wellness activities function
9. movement
10. strength
11. endurance
12. motor abilities
13. body structure
14. sensory
15. psycho-social status
16. Patient Satisfaction (patient assessment) & Patient Compliance (therapist assessment)

Special Analyses describe the absolute (means & standard deviations) and relative (correlations) relationships between various independent variables and the dependent outcomes variables, for you and the respective ATOA universe. The independent variables include:

- Duration between injury/surgery and beginning of AT treatments.
- Severity of injury.
- Previous episode?
- Comorbid factors?
- Duration of treatments.
- Number of treatments.
- Frequency of treatments.
- Percentage of treatments provided by AT.
- Reason for discharge.
- Patient gender.
- Patient age.

PROCEDURE

Pre-Proposal Submission—The NATA Foundation now requires that investigators interested in submitting a grant application to the NATA Foundation first submit a "Pre-proposal." The purpose of the Pre-proposal is to optimize the time invested by both the NATA Foundation Research Committee and the investigators in grant proposals submitted to the NATA Foundation. The Pre-proposal will allow the NATA Foundation Research Committee to evaluate whether or not the proposed research project is of interest to the NATA Foundation. The NATA Foundation Research Committee will evaluate the Pre-Proposal both for subject matter (topic and hypotheses) and for research design/methodology. Based upon this evaluation, the committee will then either invite the submission of a full proposal or indicate that the proposed project is not of interest to the NATA Foundation. An invitation to submit a full proposal does not imply a commitment to funding. It does indicate that the topic is of potential interest to the NATA Foundation and that the general research design seems reasonable based on the information given in the Pre-proposal. A commitment to funding may occur only after a detailed review of the full proposal by the NATA Foundation Research Committee.

Instructions for Submission—The pre-proposal must be submitted in both hardcopy (2 page limit, single-spaced) and 3.5" diskette. Applicants will receive results of the review within 6 weeks after the pre-proposal is received. Submission deadlines for full proposals are March 1 and September 1. The principal investigator must be explicit and concise in providing the following information:

1. Name, Credentials, Address, Phone, Fax, E-mail, Sponsoring Institution, Title of Proposal
2. Statement of the Problem. This section should contain a brief statement of the problem and should state explicitly how the project relates to athletic training and/or the healthcare of the physically active.

3. Specific Aims and Hypotheses. This section should present the specific questions to be addressed and the specific hypotheses that will be tested in the project. It is often helpful to present numbered specific aims accompanied by the associated hypotheses.
4. Experimental Design and General Methods. This section should contain a general outline of the research design of the proposed study, and should indicate what methods will be used to collect key data. There is no need to provide detailed descriptions of the methods.

Mail Completed Pre-proposal to:
Michael R. Sitler, EdD, ATC,
Chair, NATA Foundation Research Committee
Department of Kinesiology,
114 Pearson Hall
Temple University
Philadelphia, PA 19122

Appendix 6

Improve Your Bottom Line with Certified Athletic Trainers

Reprinted with permission from the National Athletic Trainers' Association.

WHO WE ARE

Certified athletic trainers (ATCs) work under the supervision of a licensed physician and specialize in the prevention, recognition, treatment and rehabilitation of injuries incurred by athletes and those engaged in physical activity. Athletic training is recognized as an allied healthcare profession by the American Medical Association, and education programs are accredited by the AMA's Commission on Accreditation of Allied Health Education Programs.

CERTIFICATION STANDARDS

Certification standards are established by the National Athletic Trainers' Association Board of Certification (NATABOC). In order to obtain certification as an athletic trainer, an individual must: possess a bachelor's degree from an accredited college or university; complete athletic training experience hours under the supervision of an NATABOC certified athletic trainer; and pass a written, practical and written simulation examination administered by the NATABOC. After an athletic trainer is certified, he or she must obtain 80 hours of continuing education units within a three-year reporting term to maintain certification.

REIMBURSEMENT

In 1996 the AMA's CPT coding division clarified that the physical medicine CPT codes are not provider specific but may be used by any provider qualified to perform the service.

In November 1999, the American Hospital Association Uniform Billing Committee expanded its 94x category titled "Other Therapeutic Services, continued." As a result, UB code 951, titled "Athletic Training," became effective October 1, 2000. The addition of this subcategory for athletic training formally recognizes the services these professionals provide. It will be beneficial for ATCs working in the hospital setting and the payers reimbursing for their services.

In July 2000, the AMA's CPT Code Editorial Panel approved the addition of athletic training evaluation/re-evaluation codes to be effective January 1, 2002. Until that time, according to the AMA, athletic trainers may use CPT code 97799 for athletic training evaluation/re-evaluation. These regulatory codes clearly define athletic training services and help facilitate billing and reimbursement.

WHY DO YOU NEED ATCS?

Certified athletic trainers provide a cost-effective continuum of care. Working as physician extenders for patients with musculoskeletal injuries, ATCs are a proven, valuable commodity. A recently published outcomes study of athletic training services illustrates the effectiveness of certified athletic trainers in treating physically active people, and it documents that certified athletic trainers provide a high level of patient satisfaction. According to the study, published in the Journal of Rehabilitation Outcomes Measurement, it is proven that "certified athletic trainers effect a change in the function and quality of life outcomes of individuals with musculoskeletal disorders." In addition, based on analysis done by an independent outcomes research company, Focus on Therapeutic Outcomes (FOTO), ATCs provide the same levels of outcome, value and patient satisfaction as physical therapists in sports medicine clinical settings.

Certified athletic trainers work in a variety of professional settings – including the "traditional setting" – such as high school, collegiate and professional sports. However, more than 8,000 certified athletic trainers (or 40% of all ATCs) are now employed in sports medicine clinics, hospitals and other treatment facilities.

THEIR VALUE TO YOU

Third party payers are recognizing the value of athletic trainers as demonstrated by their reimbursement for athletic training services. An increasing number of third party payers throughout the nation are approving reimbursement for athletic training.

Certified athletic trainers are highly skilled, versatile health care providers. Consider them when you're looking to maximize your resources and improve your bottom line.

 *Appendix 7*

Letter of Support

Dear Hospital Administrator:

My name is *John Doe, MD*. I am an *orthopedic surgeon* at *county hospital*. For the past few years I have been sending my physically active patients to certified athletic trainers for their postoperative rehabilitation. I have been very pleased with the results.

Athletic trainers are currently *licensed/certified/registered* in our state. (*Alternately, if no regulation by state: Athletic trainers are certified nationally by the National Athletic Trainers' Association Board of Certification*). They must meet stringent educational and experiential qualifications in addition to passing a *three-part* examination to receive such status (*modify exam definition to meet state requirements*).

My experience working with these individuals has found them as qualified as other allied health care professionals in the rehabilitation of musculoskeletal injuries. They are consummate professionals who work under my direction to facilitate the most effective rehabilitation strategy for my patients.

If you do not have these highly skilled professionals on staff, I urge you to consider bringing them onboard. You will not regret your decision to do so. If you do have them onboard, congratulations, you are providing your patients with a valuable tool for effective rehabilitation.

Sincerely,

John Doe, MD

The National Athletic Trainers' Association: Certified Athletic Trainers

Reprinted with permission from the National Athletic Trainers' Association

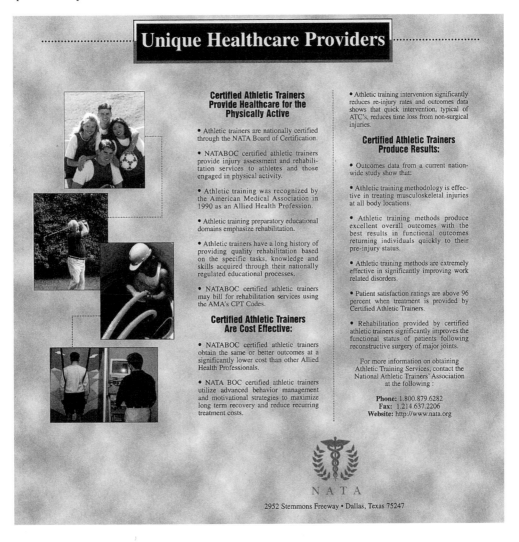

Unique Healthcare Providers

Certified Athletic Trainers Provide Healthcare for the Physically Active

• Athletic trainers are nationally certified through the NATA Board of Certification.

• NATABOC certified athletic trainers provide injury assessment and rehabilitation services to athletes and those engaged in physical activity.

• Athletic training was recognized by the American Medical Association in 1990 as an Allied Health Profession.

• Athletic training preparatory educational domains emphasize rehabilitation.

• Athletic trainers have a long history of providing quality rehabilitation based on the specific tasks, knowledge and skills acquired through their nationally regulated educational processes.

• NATABOC certified athletic trainers may bill for rehabilitation services using the AMA's CPT Codes.

Certified Athletic Trainers Are Cost Effective:

• NATABOC certified athletic trainers obtain the same or better outcomes at a significantly lower cost than other Allied Health Professionals.

• NATA BOC certified athletic trainers utilize advanced behavior management and motivational strategies to maximize long term recovery and reduce recurring treatment costs.

• Athletic training intervention significantly reduces re-injury rates and outcomes data shows that quick intervention, typical of ATC's, reduces time loss from non-surgical injuries.

Certified Athletic Trainers Produce Results:

• Outcomes data from a current nationwide study show that:

• Athletic training methodology is effective in treating musculoskeletal injuries at all body locations.

• Athletic training methods produce excellent overall outcomes with the best results in functional outcomes returning individuals quickly to their pre-injury status.

• Athletic training methods are extremely effective in significantly improving work related disorders.

• Patient satisfaction ratings are above 96 percent when treatment is provided by Certified Athletic Trainers.

• Rehabilitation provided by certified athletic trainers significantly improves the functional status of patients following reconstructive surgery of major joints.

For more information on obtaining Athletic Training Services, contact the National Athletic Trainers' Association at the following :

Phone: 1.800.879.6282
Fax: 1.214.637.2206
Website: http://www.nata.org

N A T A

2952 Stemmons Freeway • Dallas, Texas 75247

Appendix 9

The State of Georgia, House Bill 93

THE STATE OF GEORGIA
1999 GA H.B. 93
GEORGIA 145TH GENERAL ASSEMBLY – 1999-00 REGULAR SESSION
HOUSE BILL 93

H.B. NO. 93 (AS.PASSED HOUSE AND SENATE)
BY: REPRESENTATIVES WILLIAMS OF THE 114TH AND HEARD OF THE 89TH

VERSION: Enacted
VERSION-DATE: April 19, 1999
SYNOPSIS:

A BILL TO BE ENTITLED

AN ACT

To amend Title 33 of the Official Code of Georgia Annotated, relating to insurance, so as to include athletic trainers within the definition of health care providers for purposes of managed health care plans; to provide for reimbursement under insurance policies for services within the scope of practice of athletic trainers; to repeal conflicting laws; and for other purposes.

NOTICE:
[A> UPPERCASE TEXT WITHIN THESE SYMBOLS IS ADDED <A]

TEXT: BE IT ENACTED BY THE GENERAL ASSEMBLY OF GEORGIA:

SECTION 1.

Title 33 of the Official Code of Georgia Annotated, relating to insurance, is amended by striking paragraph (3) of Code Section 33-20A-3, relating to definitions relative to managed healthcare plans, and inserting in lieu thereof the following:

"(3) 'Health care provider' or 'provider' means any physician, dentist, podiatrist, pharmacist, optometrist, psychologist, clinical social worker, advance practice nurse, registered optician, licensed professional counselor, physical therapist, marriage and family therapist, chiropractor, [A> ATHLET-IC TRAINER QUALIFIED PURSUANT TO PARAGRAPH (1) OR (2) OF SUBSECTION (A) OF

CODE SECTION 43-5-8, <A] occupational therapist, speech language pathologist, audiologist, dietitian, or physician's assistant."

SECTION 2.

Said title is further amended by adding a new Code Section 33-24-27.2 to read as follows: "33-24-27.2.

(a) Notwithstanding any provision in policies or contracts which might be construed to the contrary, from and after July 1, 1999, all individual, group, or blanket policies of accident and sickness insurance and individual or group service or indemnity contracts issued by nonprofit corporations or by health care corporations which are issued, delivered, issued for delivery, amended, or renewed in this state and which provide coverage for services which are within the lawful scope of practice of an athletic trainer qualified pursuant to paragraph (1) or (2) of subsection (a) of Code Section 43-5-8 shall be deemed to provide that any person covered under such policies or contracts shall be entitled to receive reimbursement for services under such policies or contracts regardless of whether such services are rendered by a duly licensed doctor of medicine or by an athletic trainer qualified pursuant to paragraph (1) or (2) of subsection (a) of Code Section 43-5-8. Nothing contained herein shall require an insurance to offer such coverage.

(b) This Code section shall not be construed so as to impair the obligation of any policy or contract which is in existence prior to July 1, 1999."

SECTION 3.

All laws and parts of laws in conflict with this Act are repealed.

LEGAL OPINION OF HB 93

1. HB 93 was drafted and approved by the legal counsel of the State of Georgia.

2. After HB 93 was passed by the Georgia House of Representatives, a Senate committee met to review and scrutinize HB 93. This committee determined that HB 93 was worthy of accepting as law.

3. Four different legal people gave their opinions as to the meaning of HB 93, and the following information is an aggregation of those opinions. It should be noted that all four legal people arrived at the same conclusions regarding HB 93.

GEORGIA BOARD OF ATHLETIC TRAINERS HOUSE BILL 93

House Bill 93 (HB 93) was enacted by the Georgia General Assembly during its 1999 legislative session and was signed into law by Gov. Barnes on April 19, 1999.

Objectives of HB 93

1. The Bill was sponsored by Rep. Robin Williams and Rep. Keith Heard in response to difficulties raised by athletic trainers, patients, employers and insurance carriers with regard to reimbursement for services rendered to patients by an athletic trainer for diagnoses falling within their lawful scope of practice. Athletic trainers have been eligible for reimbursement, by law, since 1977. Many insurers were taking the position that only doctors and physical therapists were required to be reimbursed under their own insurance policies while other insurers were reimbursing for services delivered by an athletic trainer HB 93 was legislated to correct this misconception and to provide a remedy for the citizens of Georgia.

2. This law was legislated to clarify to employers and insurance carriers that athletic trainers had often been the provider of health care services for which other providers had been billing, and to formulate consistency across the State with regard to reimbursement of services rendered by an athletic trainer which fall within the athletic trainer's scope of practice (as defined in O.C.G.A. sec. 43-5-1). (see footnote) HB 93 was passed so that athletic trainers and their patients will no longer experience reimbursement denials and inconsistencies by insurers who otherwise reimburse physicians for the same services.

Explanation of HB 93

1. The law provides that beginning July 1, 1999, all insurance policies in the State of Georgia that provide coverage for services which are within the lawful scope of practice of athletic trainers shall be construed to provide reimbursement for such services regardless of whether the services are rendered by a doctor OR an athletic trainer. If a particular contract requires reimbursement for certain services which can be and are rendered by a duly qualified athletic trainer, then the services must be reimbursed. (A duly qualified athletic trainer is defined pursuant to O.C.G.A. sec. 13-5-8(a)(1) and (2).

This means that any health care insurance policy providing coverage for athletic injuries, (or injuries preventing athletic participation, or any injury comparable thereof as defined in O.C.G.A. 43-5-1) to individuals in the State of Georgia must reimburse such individuals when they receive treatment by an athletic trainer if a doctor of medicine would receive reimbursement for providing the same service . Indeed, if an insurance policy covers services within the lawful scope of practice of athletic trainers, HB 93 prohibits such policies from excluding patients from receiving reimbursement for services rendered by athletic trainers.

2. An insurance policy does not have to state that it specifically includes coverage for services rendered by an athletic trainer, but rather so long as the policy covers services typically and legally provided by athletic trainers, then the athletic trainer will receive reimbursement if a doctor or other provider would receive such reimbursement.

Insurance carriers may exclude coverage for certain injuries, sicknesses, or accidents, however, HB 93 prohibits them from excluding athletic trainers from reimbursement for treatment of those injuries, sicknesses or accidents if they fall within the athletic trainer scope of practice and would otherwise be reimbursed if delivered by a physician.

For example, if a patient with health insurance coverage suffers an injury to his back or fractures his ankle, and is treated by an athletic trainer within his scope of practice for such injury, such patient shall be reimbursed as a matter of law for such treatment by the athletic trainer if such treatment would also be reimbursed to a physician. This is true whether or not the insurance policy specifically mentions athletic trainers or athletic injures, so long as the policy covers care and treatment of back and ankle injuries.

3. The last sentence in Section 2 states that "nothing contained herein shall require an insurance [sic] to offer such coverage." The term "coverage" refers to the nature of injury, sickness, or accident, and not to the health care provider of the treatment for the injury, sickness or accident.

4. HB 93 amended the definition of a "health care provider" in managed health care plans across the State of Georgia so as to include athletic trainers who are qualified pursuant to O.C.G.A. sec. 43-5-8(a)(1) and (2), providing that athletic trainers are now included as a provider of health care services. (This does not mean that athletic trainers are not health care providers under other types of health care plans).

A duly qualified athletic trainer is a health care provider under managed care plans and reimbursement cannot be denies because they are athletic trainers. If a particular contract requires reimbursement for certain services which can be and are rendered by a duly qualified athletic trainer, then they must be reimbursed.

*O.C.G.A. sec. 43-5-1(1) defines an athletic injury as:

[a]ny injury sustained by a person as a result of such person's participation in exercises, sports, games, or recreation requiring physical strength, agility, flexibility, range of motion, speed, or stamina or any comparable injury which prevents such person from participating in such activities.

O.C.G.A. sec. 43-5-1(2) defines an athletic trainer as:

[a] person with specific qualifications, as set forth in Code Section 43-5-8 who, upon the advice and consent of a physician, carries out the practice of prevention, recognition, evaluation, management, disposition, treatment or rehabilitation of athletic injuries, and, in carrying out these functions, the athletic trainer is authorized to use physical modalities, such as heat, light sound, cold, electricity, or mechanical devices related to prevention, recognition, evaluation, management, disposition, rehabilitation, and treatment. The term "athletic trainer" shall not include any student, teacher, or other person who serves as an athletic trainer for an elementary school or high school, either public or private, within this state.

Note: The current Georgia Attorney General's opinion regarding the athletic trainer scope of practice is out of date. It was written in 1984. It does NOT reflect either the 1991 or HB 93 amendments to the athletic trainer law. Current law always supersedes the Attorney General's opinion.

Appendix 10

Billing Vignettes

Following are examples of services provided by licensed athletic trainers illustrating specific use of current procedural terminology (CPT) codes to describe billable services. CPT code information is in reference to CPT codes 1999. It is important to have the proper International Classification of Diseases (ICD-9) diagnosis code prior to using CPT codes.

ATHLETIC TRAINING EVALUATION

Typical Patient

A 26-year-old male with a knee injury resulting from participation in a recreational basketball game. The patient is postoperative and has a physician's order for rehabilitation/evaluate and treat.

Description of Procedure(s)/Services

A complete physical evaluation of the patient is performed by a licensed athletic trainer, including:
1. A comprehensive history detailing the present condition as well as the description of the occurrence of the trauma. Includes any past or present medical conditions and prior or present treatments for injury; allergies are established. Also includes a physical evaluation of the injury and of the status of the patient, including (if appropriate) but not limited to: visual inspection, palpation, active and passive ROM measurements, anthropometric measurements, strength testing, proprioceptive/neurological testing, functional testing, provocative testing, aerobic testing, and gait evaluation.
2. An evaluation of the patient's desired goals and motivations to return to or improve his physical abilities.
3. The origination and documentation of a comprehensive treatment, rehabilitation, and/or performance enhancement plan of care to be carried out under the direct supervision of the licensed athletic trainer.
4. Discussion of these findings in the plan of care with the patient to the mutual satisfaction of both parties. Includes timeframe for re-evaluation to assess progress of rehabilitation program.

CPT Code 97799—Unlisted Physical Medicine/Rehabilitation Service or Procedure

Used for re-evaluation by a licensed athletic trainer to determine effectiveness of plan of care and modifications needed. Specific code for athletic training evaluation will be available in 2002.

THERAPEUTIC EXERCISE

Typical Patient

An 18-year-old female with a shoulder injury resulting from participation in volleyball is diagnosed by a physician with a rotator cuff strain. The physician prescribes therapeutic exercise.

Description of Procedure(s)/Services

A licensed athletic trainer instructs the patient in specific therapeutic shoulder exercises and establishes a home exercise program.

CPT Code 97110—Therapeutic Exercise

Used when performing therapeutic exercises to develop strength and endurance, ROM, and flexibility to one or more areas (each 15 minutes). One-on-one interaction with patient. Example: Use this charge when performing initial ACL quad vmo and ROM exercises, or performing lumbar stabilization and the goal is strengthening muscles.

PHYSICAL PERFORMANCE TESTING

Typical Patient

A 16-year-old female basketball player has been diagnosed by a physician with patellofemoral malalignment. The physician orders specific muscle strength and endurance testing to determine current muscular status to be able to prescribe appropriate therapeutic exercises.

Description of Procedure(s)/Services

A licensed athletic trainer performs specific lower extremity muscular strength and endurance tests utilizing manual muscle testing techniques as well as conventional muscle testing devices and provides written reports of findings to the diagnosing physician.

CPT Code 97750—Physical Performance Test

Used when performing specific musculoskeletal examinations, such as specific muscle strength, closed chain testing, vestibular/balance testing, isokinetic testing, and other physical performance testing. Must have a written report/documentation to support this (eg, physician progress report for patient visit). Also used for functional capacity evaluations (each 15 minutes).

TAPING

Typical Patient

A 19-year-old male football player is diagnosed by a physician with a second-degree lateral right ankle sprain. The physician prescribes supportive adhesive strapping as part of the treatment plan.

Description of Procedure(s)/Services

A licensed athletic trainer provides an adhesive ankle strapping/taping support to the injured ankle during the patient's treatment session.

CPT Code 97139—Taping (Each Visit)

Charge for taping of patient during treatment session, taping shoulder, knee, ankle, etc, or more specifically: 29540—Ankle Strapping/Taping.

ULTRASOUND

Typical Patient

A 30-year-old male recreational basketball player is diagnosed by a physician with a quadriceps muscle strain. The physician prescribes ultrasound treatment.

Description of Procedure(s)/Services

A licensed athletic trainer performs the ultrasound treatment.

CPT Code 97035—Ultrasound (Each 15 Minutes)

Deep heat modality used to decrease pain and muscle spasm.

HOT PACKS

Typical Patient

A 45-year-old female with low back pain resulting from participation in a weight-training program is diagnosed by a physician with chronic low back pain. As part of the treatment plan, the physician prescribes moist heat treatment in conjunction with therapeutic exercise.

Description of Procedure(s)/Services

A licensed athletic trainer applies moist heat pack treatments prior to instructing the patient in therapeutic exercise.

CPT Code 97010—Hot Packs (Application to One or More Areas)

Application of moist heat pack used for pain modulation muscle relaxation. Can only bill for this if used in conjunction with another therapy treatment or modality. Charged by the visit.

Glossary

Agency for Health Care Policy and Research (AHCPR): The agency of the Public Health Service responsible for enhancing the quality, appropriateness, and effectiveness of health care services. The agency was created by Congress in 1989 to engage in quality improvement-related activities, including development of peer-reviewed outcomes studies and practice parameters.

Ambulatory care: Health care services provided on an outpatient basis. No overnight stay in a hospital is required. The services of ambulatory care centers, hospital outpatient departments, physicians' offices, and home health care services fall under this heading.

Balanced Budget Act of 1997: Legislation that provided cost containment in Medicare program; mandated a shift from fee-for-service to prospective payment system for long-term care facilities and capped therapy benefits under Medicare Part B reimbursement. Required implementation of prospective payment systems for patients in skilled nursing facilities covered by Medicare Part A (Resource Utilization Groups System III) and Medicare Part B (fee schedules).

Beneficiary: Individual who is either using or eligible to use insurance benefits, including health insurance benefits, under an insurance contract.

Benefit payment schedule: List of amounts an insurance plan will pay for covered health care services.

Benefit: The payment for or health care services provided under terms of a contract with a managed care organization.

Bundled pricing: A packaging of medical services that may include all of the services required for a certain diagnosis.

Capitation: A payment system whereby managed care plans pay health care providers a fixed amount to care for a patient over a given period. Providers are not reimbursed for services that exceed the allotted amount. The rate may be fixed for all members, or it can be adjusted for the age and gender of the member based on actuarial projections of medical utilization.

Case management: The process by which all health-related matters of a case are managed by a physician, nurse, or designated health professional.

Case rate: A flat fee paid for a client's treatment based on his or her diagnosis and/or presenting problem. For this fee, the provider covers all of the services the client requires for a specific period of time, also known as a bundled rate or flat fee per case.

Claims review: The method by which an enrollee's health care service claims are reviewed prior to reimbursement. The purpose is to validate the medical necessity of the provided services and to be sure the cost of the service is not excessive.

Coinsurance: A cost-sharing requirement under a health insurance policy that provides that the insured will assume a portion or percentage of the costs of covered services. After the deductible is paid, this provision forces the subscriber to pay for a certain percentage of any remaining medical bills, usually 20%.

Commercial payers: Third-party payers other than government-sponsored health care plans.

Comprehensive outpatient rehabilitation facilities (CORFs): Private rehabilitation practices that have met Medicare guidelines and are certified by the Health Care Financing Administration as a Medicare provider.

Copayment: A type of cost-sharing that requires the insured or subscriber to pay a specified flat dollar amount, usually on a per unit of service basis, with the third-party payer reimbursing some portion of remaining charges.

Current procedural terminology (CPT): A uniform coding system for therapy services that is used to determine provider fee schedule reimbursement.

Deductible: The out-of-pocket expenses that must be borne by an insurance subscriber before the insurer will begin reimbursing the subscriber for additional expenses.

Diagnosis-related groups (DRG): A system used by Medicare and other insurers to classify illnesses according to diagnosis and treatment. All Medicare inpatient hospital operating costs are determined in advance and paid on a per-case basis, according to a fixed amount or weight established for each DRG.

Discounted fee-for-service: An agreed-upon rate for service between the provider and payer that is usually less than the provider's full fee. This may be a fixed amount per service or a percentage discount. Providers generally accept such contracts because they represent a means to increase their volume or reduce their chances of losing volume.

Exclusive provider organization (EPO): A health care plan in which a group of providers contract with an insurer, employer, or third-party administrator to agree to provide care at a negotiated level of reimbursement. Members must seek services from participating providers in order to obtain reimbursement.

Fee-for-service: The traditional form of health care provider billing whereby the provider charges the patient and/or third-party payer based on a fee schedule set for each service provided.

Gatekeeper: A physician (usually primary care) selected by the participant, who establishes a treatment plan, decides need for referral, and whose function is to reduce health care utilization and costs.

Health Care Financing Administration (HCFA): Federal agency that regulates and administrates the Medicare program.

Health Care Professionals Advisory Committee (HCPAC): Committee of the American Medical Association made up of representatives from allied health care professions.

Health maintenance organization (HMO): An organized group of health care providers that delivers a defined set of health care services to an enrolled population. Payment for the services is usually prepaid with a fixed sum of money. Choice of providers is usually limited to the HMO network physicians and hospitals.

Health Plan Employer Data and Information Set (HEDIS): A manner in which managed care plans are evaluated on measures including quality, member satisfaction, utilization, and financial stability.

Indemnity health insurance: A traditional health insurance plan with little or no benefit management, a fee-for-service reimbursement model, and few restrictions on provider selection.

Independent physicians association (IPA): A group of physician providers who contract to provide services for managed care organization (MCO) clients or the MCO itself.

Integrated delivery system (IDS): A system by which providers combine resources and services to defined populations. This is usually done to become more attractive to managed care groups and in some cases as part of a managed care structure.

International Classification of Diseases (ICD-9) diagnosis codes: Codes utilized to identify and describe medical diagnoses.

Managed care incentives: Rewards given to providers and participants for reduced health care utilization and cost containment.

Managed care organization (MCO): A preplanned health care delivery system that integrates financing and delivery of health care services to participating groups and/or individuals. The goal of managed care is to deliver quality health care while containing costs.

Medicare: The government health care plan for the elderly, 65 years of age or older.

National Committee on Quality Assurance (NCQA): A nonprofit organization created to improve patient care quality and health plan performance in partnership with managed care plans, purchasers, consumers, and the public sector.

National Uniform Billing Committee (NUBC): A committee under the auspices of the American Hospital Association whose function is to establish and modify uniform billing codes.

Outcomes management: A technology of patient experience designed to help patients, payers, and providers make more rational medical care-related choices based on better insight into the effect of these choices on the patient's life.

Point-of-service (POS) plan: A health care plan in which members receive care provided by a network of participating providers, but have the option of obtaining care outside the network. Many refer to this type of plan as one of the many hybrid managed care plans.

Preauthorization: A method of monitoring and controlling utilization by evaluating the need for medical service prior to it being performed.

Preferred provider organization (PPO): An organized group of health care providers contracted to deliver health care services to a defined population. Payment to the providers in the PPO is usually discounted. Members may utilize providers outside of the network, but increased copayments are required.

Premium: Money paid out in advance for insurance coverage.

Quality assurance (QA), quality management (QM), continuous quality improvement (CQI): Activities and programs intended to ensure the quality of care in a defined medical setting. Such programs include peer or utilization review components to identify and remedy deficiencies in quality. The program must have a mechanism for assessing its effectiveness and may measure care against pre-established standards.

Self-insurance: The practice of an employer or organization assuming responsibility for health care losses of its employees. This usually includes setting up a fund against which claim payments are drawn. Claims processing is often handled through an administrative services contract with an independent organization.

Third-party administrator: Individual or company that contracts with employers who want to self-insure the health of their employees. They develop and coordinate self-insurance programs, process and pay the claim, and may help locate stop-loss insurance for the employer. They can also analyze the effectiveness of the program and trace the patterns of those using the benefits.

Third-party payer: An organization, agency, or company responsible for payment of health care services utilized by an individual or individuals who are members of the specific plan.

Uniform billing (UB) code: American Hospital Association-approved codes used to describe health care services provided in hospital facilities. Used for billing purposes.

Unique Physician Identification Number (UPIN): Identification number issued by the Health Care Financing Administration to identify physicians who treat Medicare patients.

Usual, customary, and reasonable (UCR): A reimbursement method whereby a health insurance plan pays a physician's full charge if it is reasonable and does not exceed his or her usual charges and the amount customarily charged for the service by other physicians in the area.

Utilization: The patterns of use of a service or type of service within a specified time. Utilization is usually expressed in rate per unit of population-at-risk for a given period (eg, the number of hospital admissions per year per 1000 people enrolled in an HMO).

Utilization review (UR): A systematic means for reviewing and controlling patients' use of medical services as well as the appropriateness and quality of that care. UR usually involves data collection, review, and/or authorization, especially for services such as specialist referrals, emergency room use, and hospitalization.

Index

A

access to care, 5
administrative costs, 6
American Medical Association (AMA)
    current procedural terminology codes
        (CPT), 37–38, 119
    early opposition to managed care, 2
    recognition of athletic training, 11, 20
appeal process, 49
appropriateness of service, 48
ATC. see certified athletic trainer
athletic training evaluation CPT code,
    133–134
athletic training outcomes assessment, 23
ATOA. see athletic training outcomes
    assessment

B

billing
    itemized statement, 66–67
    mistakes, 51
    for soft goods, 67
    uniform codes, 16
billing codes. see current procedural
    terminology codes
Blue Cross insurance plans, 1–2
    UB-92 claim form, 43, 46

C

capitation, 5, 6, 55, 56
certified athletic trainers
    and bottom line, 119–120
    certification standards, 99
    as nonphysician provider, 13
    overlap with physical therapy, 59
    payer recognition of, 75
    as physician extenders, 58–59, 61, 83
    professional profile, 99
    recognition by AMA, 11
    recognition by Medicare, 13–14
    regulations governing, 59
    settings for, 56
    success and recognition by Medicare, 14
    uniqueness of service, 75
certified outpatient rehabilitation facility
    (CORF), 56
    billing for athletic training services, 58–59
claim forms, 43
claims
    completeness of, 48–49
    denial, 47–49
    electronic billing, 51–52
    filing, 37, 47
claims filing
    billing mistakes, 51
    electronic billing, 51–52
client support, 78
clinical setting
    billing for athletic training services, 58–59
    and business ethics, 59
    future of reimbursement, 60
    outreach services, 57–58
    and reimbursement history, 56–57
codes. see current procedural terminology
    codes (CPT)
    American Hospital Association UB code
        951, 119
collegiate setting
    billing issues, 68–69
    and future of reimbursement, 84
    itemized statement, 66–67

letter to parents, 64–65
Missouri registration functional protocol, 61
outcomes research data, 108
reimbursement models, 60
reports, 62–63
variations of reimbursement models, 65
communication with third-party payers, 50
community rating methods, 2
compliance, 49
consultants, 26, 27
CORF. see certified outpatient rehabilitation facility (CORF)
corporate settings. see industrial setting
cost-benefit analysis, 76
cost of health care
    administrative, 6
    reduction methods by MCOs, 5
    rise through decades, 3
CPT. see current procedural terminology codes (CPT)
current procedural terminology codes (CPT), 15–16, 37–38
for athletic training services, 119
examples, 38
for hospital setting, 58
hot packs, 135
physical performance testing, 134
taping, 134–135
therapeutic exercise, 134
ultrasound, 135
unlisted physical medicine service, 133–134

D

deductible, 5
demonstration projects, 14, 77
denial of payment, 47–49
disease classification. see International Classification of Diseases
documentation, 42–43
    patient encounter form, 44
    reports, 62–63
Dunn, Ron, 57

E

effectiveness of medical care. see outcomes research
EHOs, 8
electronic billing, 51–52

in Missouri collegiate setting, 60
EPOs (exclusive provider organizations), 7
ethical business practices, 59
experience rating methods, 2

F

federal government
    and future of health care, 8
    role in reimbursement, 2–3
    valuation of prevention, 14–15
fee-for-service indemnity plans, 2
    and medical care costs, 3
    and role of certified athletic trainer, 13
fee-for-service reimbursement, 55
    incidents of, 57
    in industrial settings, 70–71
filing a claim. see claims filing
fluctuation, 6
focus group, 32
Focus on Therapeutic Outcomes (FOTO), 25, 77, 120
Forbis, Pat, 57
function, definition, 103

G

gag clauses, 8
gatekeeper, 5
Georgia
    house bill 93, 127–130
    legislation for reimbursement, 99
    state insurance code legislation, 80
Georgia Tech reimbursement, 65
government
    federal
        and future of health care, 8
        role in reimbursement, 2–3
        valuation of prevention, 14–15
    state
        and challenges to reimbursement, 13
        licensed, certified, or registered, 16
        reimbursement advisory groups, 21

H

HCFA-1500, 45
HCFA-1500 claim form, 43
health care insurance. see insurance
Health Care Practitioner Advisory Council (HCPAC), 16
    and Medicare recognition, 26

recognition of athletic training, 85
recognition of clinical facilities, 58
health maintenance organizations (HMOs), 2
health-related quality of life (HRQL), 103,
    104–105
high school. see secondary school setting
Hill-Burton Act, 3
HMOs, 7
hospital setting, 58
Hospital Survey and Construction Act, 3
hot packs CPT code, 135
HRQL, 103

I

ICD. see International Classification of
    Diseases
IDS (integrated delivery system), 6, 8
independent practice association (IPA), 5
industrial setting, 69–70
    billing for services, 70–71
    contact persons, 91
    and future of reimbursement, 84–85
    outcomes research data, 108
inpatient services, 4
insurance
    claim forms, 43
    history of, 1–2
    state code legislation, 80
insurance companies
    history of recognizing athletic trainers, 27
    list of recognized carriers, 90
    meetings with, 90–91
    outcomes research data, 109–110
    Power Point presentation to, 91
International Classification of Diseases, 38, 63
itemized statement, 66–67

J

Joint Commission on Sports Medicine and
    Science, 79

L

legal issues, 90
legislation
    Georgia house bill 93, 127–130
    Medicare reimbursement, 78, 80
licensed, 16

M

managed care
    consultant, 26
    cost reduction methods, 5–6
    early history of, 2
    growth of, 3
    outcomes research data, 109–110
    revenues, 4
    role of NCQA, 16
marketing, 76–77
Massachusetts and reimbursement, 56
Medicaid
    formation of, 3
    outcomes research data, 109–110
    recognition of athletic training, 13–14
Medicare
    Balanced Budget Act of 1997, 137
    and billing for services in clinical setting,
        58
    demonstration projects, 14
    formation of, 3
    HCFA-1500 claim form, 43, 45
    legislation for reimbursement, 78, 80
    letter concerning regulatory issues, 95–96
    outcomes research data, 109–110
    recent changes in reimbursement policies,
        8
    recognition of athletic training, 13–14, 26
Missouri
    registration functional protocol, 61
    reimbursement, 57, 60
modalities
    current procedural terminology codes
        (CPT) for, 41–42
    most effective, 24

N

NATA
    association profile, 100
    certification standards, 99, 119
    information poster, 125
    membership statistics, 12
    mission statement, 11
    objectives, 20
    outcomes research report database,
        114–115
    outcomes research RFP, 115–116

NATA Reimbursement Advisory Group
consultants, 26, 27, 29
education of membership, 25
efforts toward reimbursement, 85
focus group, 32
history of, 19
information packet, 20
members in 2000, 29–32
original members, 20
outcomes research, 22–24
public relations plan, 29
reimbursement strategies, 27
as resource, 91
revised mission and goals, 27–29
states for further study, 25–26
National Athletic Trainers' Association. see
NATA
National Committee for Quality Assurance
(NCQA), 16
nonphysician providers, 13, 16

O

Occupational Safety and Health
Administration (OSHA), 69
opposition to reimbursement, 80
outcomes research, 21
for athletic training services
data, 107
data availability, 113
data by payer, 109–110
data by setting, 108
data collection, 23
materials and methods, 104–105
patient demographics, 106
patient satisfaction rating form, 105
publication of results, 25
request for proposals, 113–119
results, 23–24, 106
sample size, 108
scope of research, 103
statistical analysis, 106
benefits of, 23
creative use of data, 76–77
evaluation tools, 113
Focus on Therapeutic Outcomes (FOTO),
25, 120
goals, 22
outpatient services, 4

P

paperwork. see documentation
patient records, 42–43
patients
demographics for outcomes study, 106
satisfaction rating form, 105
as source of outcome information,
103–104, 113–114
payers. see third-party payers
payment methods, 55
per member per month (PMPM) payment,
6, 55
per visit reimbursement, 55
physical performance testing CPT code, 134
physical therapy
and cosigned treatments, 65
outcome comparison to athletic training,
77
overlap with athletic training, 59
and role of certified athletic trainer, 58
physician
alliances with, 77–78
letter of support, 123
relationship to certified athletic trainer, 13
physician-hospital organizations (PHOs), 8
physician-owned clinic, 58
PMPM (per member per month)
reimbursement, 6
point-of-service plans, 7
Power Point presentation, 91
PPOs (preferred provider organizations), 7
precertification, 48
premiums, 4
prevention, 14–15, 84
primary care physician, 5
procedural terminology codes. see current
procedural terminology codes (CPT)
profit
in sports medicine departments, 12
usual, customary, and reasonable rates, 3
profit sharing, 71
prospective payment, 55
providers, 3–4, 15, 38
public demand for athletic training services,
60
public relations, 29

Q

quality of care, 7, 21

R

RAG. see NATA Reimbursement Advisory Group
registration functional protocol, 61
reimbursement
    consultants, 26
    definition, 37
    evidence of, 76
    history of, 1–2
    by hourly rate, 71
    lobbying for change in government policies, 15
    methods of, 55
    NATA efforts towards, 85
    NATA recommendations for requesting, 33
    payers for athletic training services, 57
    per member per month (PMPM), 6
    state laws and, 13
    trends in, 8
Reimbursement Advisory Group. see NATA Reimbursement Advisory Group
    reinsurance, 4
    reports, 62–63
    request for proposals, 113–116
    research. see outcomes research
    retrospective payment, 55
    risk sharing, 6
    Rogers, Richard, 91

S

satisfaction rating form, 105
secondary school setting. see settings for athletic trainers
settings for athletic trainers, 56
    clinical
        billing practices, 58–59
        and business ethics, 59
        future of reimbursement, 60
        and reimbursement history, 56–57
    collegiate
        billing for soft goods, 67
        billing issues, 68–69
        and future of reimbursement, 84
        itemized statement, 66–67
        letter to parents, 64–65
        Missouri registration functional protocol, 61
        reports, 62–63
        variations of reimbursement models, 65
    industrial, 69–70, 84–85
        contact persons, 91
    outcomes research data, 108
    secondary school, 67, 84
    traditional, 60–61
SF-36, 104
SOAP notes, 43, 63
soft goods, 67
sports medicine clinics
    outcomes research data, 108
    outreach services, 57–58
state government
    and challenges to reimbursement, 13
    legislation, 25–26
    licensed, certified, or registered, 16
    reimbursement advisory groups, 21
    scope of practice act, 90
statement, itemized, 66–67
states
    Georgia
        house bill 93, 127–130
        legislation for reimbursement, 99
    Georgia Tech reimbursement, 65
    insurance code legislation, 80
    lobbying for reimbursement, 75
    Massachusetts and reimbursement, 56
    Missouri and reimbursement, 57, 60, 61
    organizing at state level, 89
    for RAG study, 25–26
    regulations governing athletic trainers, 59
    reimbursement strategies, 27
    seeking athletic trainer regulation, 99
    submitting a claim. see claims filing

T

taping CPT code, 134–135
terminology. see current procedural terminology codes (CPT)
therapeutic exercise CPT code, 134
therapist, AMA definition of, 15
third-party payers
    approaching, 57, 90
    communication with, 50
    outcomes research data, 109–110

recognition of athletic training, 75
third-party reimbursement. see
    reimbursement
traditional setting, 60–61, 84. see also
    collegiate setting

U

UB-92 claim form, 43, 46
ultrasound CPT code, 135

uniform billing (UB) codes, 16
    American Hospital Association UB code
        951, 119
unlisted procedure code, 133–134

W

withholds, 6
worker's compensation, 109–110
workplace setting. see industrial setting

BUILD *Your Library*

This book and many others on numerous different topics are available from SLACK Incorporated. For further information or a copy of our latest catalog, contact us at:

Professional Book Division
SLACK Incorporated
6900 Grove Road
Thorofare, NJ 08086 USA
Telephone: 1-856-848-1000
1-800-257-8290
Fax: 1-856-853-5991
E-mail: orders@slackinc.com
www.slackbooks.com

We accept most major credit cards and checks or money orders in US dollars drawn on a US bank. Most orders are shipped within 72 hours.

Contact us for information on recent releases, forthcoming titles, and bestsellers. If you have a comment about this title or see a need for a new book, direct your correspondence to the Editorial Director at the above address.

Thank you for your interest and we hope you found this work beneficial.

Expand Your Library
With These Exceptional Texts!

Other Exciting Books in the Athletic Training Library *Include:*

Title	Author	Book #	Price
❑ Professional Behaviors in Athletic Training	Hannam	44094	$24.00
❑ The Athletic Trainer's Guide to Strength and Endurance Training	Wiksten	44310	$24.00
❑ Current Topics in Musculoskeletal Approach: A Case Study Approach	DeCarlo	44345	$24.00
❑ Research in Athletic Training	Ingersoll	44396	$24.00

Subtotal $_____
NJ and CA Sales Tax* $_____
Handling Charge $ 4.50
Total $_____

Name: _____

Address: _____

City: _____ State: _____ Zip Code: _____

Phone: _____ Fax: _____

Charge my: ❑ [American Express] ❑ [MasterCard] ❑ [VISA] Account#: _____

Exp. date: _____ Signature: _____

Prices are subject to change. Shipping charges may apply.
*Purchases in NJ and CA are subject to tax. Please add applicable state and local taxes.

CODE:4A687

Mail Order Form To: SLACK Incorporated
Professional Book Division
6900 Grove Road
Thorofare, NJ 08086-9864

Call: 800-257-8290 or 856-848-1000
Fax: 856-853-5991
Email: Orders@slackinc.com

Visit Our World Wide Web: www.slackbooks.com